Joan Becker has a ⬚erous spi⬚ ⬚ in this
book. By sharing ⬚mily's ⬚perie⬚ ⬚ggling
with mental illr⬚ ⬚el less alone. That's a tremen⬚ ⬚ishment
when the illnes⬚ ⬚ses feelings of isolation and hopelessnes⬚ ⬚or parents
who are despera⬚ ⬚ help their suffering child. The mental health system
can and should be better, and this book inspires all of us to do everything
we can to make it so.

U.S. Sen. Chuck Grassley (R-IA)

In *Sentenced to Life*, Joan Becker masterfully leads the reader through her
family's experience with schizophrenia. From the expectations and dreams
of two young parents, through the horror of a son's mental deterioration,
and finally to the violent tragedy that took a life, Becker is open and honest.
Throughout the story her faith is front and center and a common theme is
apparent: God offers us hope that transcends all circumstances, no matter
how destructive those circumstances may be. This book is a must read for
any person who has a loved one struggling with mental illness.

Matthew S. Stanford, PhD
CEO, Hope and Healing Center & Institute
Author of *Grace for the Afflicted: A Clinical and Biblical Perspective on Mental Illness*

What Joan Becker has done by sharing the most personal and difficult
time in her life is not just courageous but will help bring hope and healing
to so many families who experience mental illness. This is an issue that
touches all of us in one way or another, and her work can help save lives.

Maura Mandt
Executive Producer, ESPY Awards

Families of loved ones with mental illness closely followed the tragedy—
the loss of Coach Thomas, the loss of a young man to a devastating
disease, and the loss of the young man again, when his illness was not
understood and he was sentenced to prison for the rest of his life. Joan
is living the heartbreak that haunts families who know this could easily
happen to them. We must all speak out for better mental health care; we
must demand it. Joan movingly sets the stage for this movement.

Teresa Bomhoff
National Alliance on Mental Illness, Greater Des Moines President

SENTENCED TO
LIFE

The Mark Becker Story

SENTENCED TO
LIFE

Mental Illness, Tragedy,
and Transformation

JOAN BECKER

This book is dedicated to every person who lives with mental illness, whether in themselves or a loved one, and especially to my son, Mark Becker, who is determined to make the best of his life each and every day.

Thank you to my own and Dave's families, as well as to my church family, community, coworkers, and friends who have supported us every step of the way. Mom and Dad, I continue to be amazed at your love and support of Mark and of our family in spite of the pain you have endured.

My love and appreciation go to my husband, David, for standing by me throughout the years (35 and counting). Thank you to my sons and their sweethearts, Brad and Jackie and Scott and Nikki, for their continued encouragement of my public speaking and writing of this book. Finally, a special thanks to my sisters, Jane and Sheryl, for listening, reading, and crying with me throughout this book project. Your wisdom and support kept me going!

God is my Rock and my Salvation, and it is only through his grace and mercy that I can survive this life's journey.

For from him and through him and to him are all things. To him be the glory forever! Amen.

—*Romans 11:36*

CONTENTS

PROLOGUE

The air is heavy. It assaults all of my senses. My eyes struggle to cut through the murky mass, and I can't seem to focus my vision. If I could only rise above it, like when a plane takes off and flies up and up and up, finally shattering through the clouds into the brilliant blue sky and sunshine.

My hands and face feel clammy from the thick soggy air. I rinse my face and neck with cool refreshing water but it provides only a brief respite until, again, I feel hot and sticky. My head is filled with a mind-numbing pressure that I cannot escape. It is eerily quiet; almost as if the birds of the air, the sheep, and my beagles seem to sense something making its way toward me just beyond the horizon. The typically fresh-smelling country air carries a slight putrid smell. What on earth is coming my way?

Wait, I'm sensing a slight shift. Is that a breeze starting to move in? I see and hear the leaves on the trees begin to blow and the branches begin to dance in the wind. The wind is picking up now, and I think, "Wonderful, maybe this overwhelming heaviness enveloping me will finally blow out of here." Will I finally find peace from this oppressiveness that has been with me so very long?

The howling wind is definitely getting louder and stronger. I start to fear this is more than a passing storm. The trees are thrashing every which way. Branches are starting to fall around me. The light gray clouds have transformed into black rolling masses. Rain is starting to pummel sharp pellets against my skin. I can't seem to escape!

Where can I seek safety and peace from this roller coaster overcoming me?

Help me, I feel like I'm being buried and can't claw my way out!

Suddenly I'm overtaken and thrown to the ground. I groan in pain. I didn't see it coming. I never anticipated this massive tsunami, this tidal wave, this earthquake, this tornado, this hurricane!

My world stops. Everything is black. The quiet is deafening. Has the storm passed? I feel life seeping back into me. I'm starting to remember it all . . . the tempest that hit without warning. Oh God, how will I ever survive the aftermath? How will I overcome the devastation? Will the sun ever shine for me again? Do I have to face this alone? Will I ever find the light beyond this storm?

MEET THE FAMILY

Everyone faces storms in life. Our family has survived two storms of unparalleled proportions. Both storms rocked our community and our lives to the core. The first, a natural disaster, wrecked our small town, catalyzing the community to pull together and rebuild both structures and lives. Just over twelve months later, another major disaster hit. We didn't see it coming, and we didn't know that our son, Mark, would be at the epicenter of that second fateful storm.

I was terrified when I started attending a new high school at the age of sixteen. How could my dad take a new job and move us away from the farm we grew up on and away from all of my cousins and friends? As I walked into my first class that morning, I met Mr. Thomas. He made a point of walking up to my twin sister and me and introducing himself. It was his first day too as a teacher at Parkersburg High School. He seemed just as nervous as we were.

Coach Thomas began a tradition that year which characterized his life priorities of faith, family, and football—not just in our school but in the entire community. Many people think he was just about football, but it was way more than that. Coach had a way of turning high school boys into men of honor, dignity, and respect. He had a knack for pulling the absolute most out of his players, both on the field and in the classroom. As my husband would attest, practices were beyond hard work but somehow Coach made the players *want* to be there. He cared about them deeply. In fact, Coach was quite instrumental in letting me know he thought Dave Becker, one of his senior football captains, would be a great person for me to get to know. Yes, he meddled! And before you know it, Coach was asking me every Friday, "Is Dave ready for the game?" Perhaps I was a bit flippant with him when I responded, "I don't know. Ask him."

I ended up marrying Dave Becker, my high school sweetheart, and it was a storybook beginning when we purchased his grandparent's house in our small hometown of Parkersburg, Iowa. Although we didn't know everyone in our community, it sure felt like we did. Three of our neighbors were ninety and older so when these newlyweds moved in, it gave the neighborhood quite a stir. In fact, Dave's great-uncle Earl, our next-door neighbor, called the police when we were on our honeymoon because of "intruders" breaking into our house. Our *friends* did a small home makeover to welcome us home: the typical Jell-O in the tub, Saran Wrap over the toilet seat, and confetti all over the place.

Our local barber, Tommy, and his wife, Sue, lived across the street from us. Tommy is one of those icons in the community. Everyone knows him and everyone loves him. Tom and Sue welcomed us to the neighborhood and, after our boys were born, they enjoyed seeing our little ones outside playing.

Just down the block lived our close friends, the Kalkwarfs and their two boys. What memories our two families have made over the years.

It took a while before I could convince Dave that there would never be a "right" time to begin a family but three years after saying "I do," Brad was born. Brad was my textbook baby. He ate, slept, and loved the attention he received as a firstborn child. We had a pretty good routine down: wake up, eat, take a walk, visit the neighbor, eat lunch, take a nap, play outside, eat supper with daddy, play with daddy, bath time, read a story, and bedtime. I figured I had learned everything about raising a baby with our firstborn. But I was soon to find out that I was quite naïve.

Take Two: It's a Different Scene

Only twenty-one months later, Mark arrived on the scene. As I read through Mark's baby book years later, I'm reminded about that first day home. Mark cried, Brad cried, my mother cried, and, of course, I cried. You mothers out there all know what I'm talking about. I had this glowing picture in my mind of one big happy family and it doesn't always quite work out that way.

Mark was a colicky child for about the first eight months of his life. I was overwhelmed with a feeling of failure as a mother when I tried everything I could think of to comfort Mark. Nothing worked. My mother-in-law (whom I loved dearly) thought it was surely something I was doing wrong. After spending a few days helping us, she handed Mark to me, sheepishly admitting, "I don't know what to do." I spent many hours lying on the couch, Mark on my stomach, staring into those dark brown eyes that seemed to bore right through my soul and, every so often, Mark would escape the pain and find rest.

Mark was just under nine months old when he ventured away from the safety of the couch and chairs and started toddling on his own. Once he started walking nothing was going to stop him and he finally found relief from his colic. This little rascal loved to climb, and every time we turned around, he was scrambling up onto something—the couch, the dining room table, the chairs, or the kitchen counter. As he grew older, he expanded his climbing ventures to trees and buildings. Mark had no fear!

By Mark's first birthday we were bursting at the seams of our home. Although we loved our small town, the neighborhood, and our family walks to the creamery, the swimming pool, the park, and neighbors, Dave and I reminisced of our childhood days growing up on the farm. We dreamed of providing our boys that same peaceful rural setting.

One Father's Day, we invited my mom and dad over for noon lunch after church. We ate a huge meal and the house became uncommonly quiet as both Brad and Mark cooperated by taking naps simultaneously. I thought perhaps I could talk my folks into taking a siesta so Dave and I could take a quick motorcycle ride. I love my parents, and they remembered what it was like raising six kids very close in age, so off we rode into the sunset. Well, not quite a sunset, but into the sun anyway.

As we were riding our 1972 350 Honda, we spotted a "For Sale" sign by the home of our dreams. Our vision of raising our boys in the country became a reality a few months later. The forty-acre property in rural Iowa boasted ten acres of trees, pastures, and natural springs, which would eventually feed into a one-acre pond stocked with large-mouth bass, bluegill, and catfish. A small flock of sheep and baby lambs each year gave the boys a small taste of the farm life we so fondly remembered.

At three years old, Mark continued to grow in his energy and enthusiasm for life. One hot, hazy summer day our friends, the Kalkwarfs, visited the farm and the kids decided to play hide and seek. Eventually, we noticed the kids had grown weary of playing their game, but Mark was missing.

We all started searching the farm and calling out his name. Since our farm had forty acres of fields, trees, streams, and pastures, my gut started to churn after about an hour of hunting with no results. As we gathered by the house and tried to get a game plan in place, I thought I heard a slight noise, sort of like murmuring. I called out Mark's name and heard a muffled cry from the trunk of our car. I was almost dizzy from the heat and fear as we opened the trunk and there was Mark, stripped down to his skivvies, sweating, beet red and hot, but he had a smile on his face. In Mark's three-year-old wisdom he thought the car trunk would be a great place to hide from the rest of the kids. Chalk it up to one more life experience for Mark and another moment of panic for Mom and Dad.

By the time Brad and Mark were both attending elementary school, I was working part-time at the high school. It made it convenient for the boys to hop on the sidewalk behind the elementary school, follow it down the hill, cross the street, and climb the flight of steps up another hill to join me after school each day. The teachers loved having them around. I'll never forget when Coach Thomas outfitted them with old football helmets and shoulder pads. Look out! A football team was in the making!

Just shy of Mark's seventh birthday, our third son, Scott, was born. Everyone seemed to think he was a surprise, but the surprise was on them when we explained, "No, we just wanted to have another baby." I think back now and realize

God had a very special purpose for our third son. Brad and Mark were excited about having a baby brother. It was so sweet when they took Scott to school for "show and tell." His big brothers were active in school, had started playing little league baseball, and were involved in various other activities.

As Mark ventured through his elementary years, he developed quite a love of drawing. I know every parent thinks their kid's art is amazing, but I will say, Mark's art was incredible and it still brings me joy. Mark was also becoming quite an athlete. I'm sure this had nothing to do with all of the climbing, running, and energy he had been born with.

I think every mom and dad look back at a certain point in life and sometimes wish it "could have been frozen in time." For me, that time was probably when Brad was in eighth grade, Mark was in sixth grade, and Scott was in elementary school. Even though the middle school years were when the boys thought it was no longer cool to turn to Mom with life's worries, it was still a great time in our family's journey. Mark had an advantage when starting sixth grade at nearby Aplington since Brad had paved the way two years earlier. Mark was able to scope out the middle school when he attended Brad's concerts, basketball games, wrestling meets, and art shows.

Mark's class was a tight-knit group and they didn't let anything stand in their way of jumping into activities and meeting new friends. Mark and his friends were always getting together to play basketball, watch movies, and just hang out. Even though they were in middle school they didn't stop having their birthday parties, scavenger hunts, church hay rides, and roller-skating nights. When Mark was planning a birthday party he didn't want anyone to feel left out. He could never narrow down the guest list below fifteen or so friends because who, after all, would he *not* invite?

Although Dave and I loved following Brad and Mark's activities at the middle school, there were many times I threatened to pound a "For Sale" sign at the end of the driveway. Between running to events and trying to keep up with the shuttle bus schedule, it was a zoo! We didn't begrudge Mark's involvement in school activities and sports given his energy level. He enjoyed the hustle and bustle of Student Council, music, band, football, basketball, track, and baseball.

The summer before his seventh grade year, Mark accepted Christ as his personal Savior at Camp Koinonia, a Bible camp located just a couple miles from our home. Soon after that momentous decision in his life, I'll never forget seeing Mark and Scott sitting on the couch together and reading verses from the Bible about salvation. Mark led his younger brother to Christ and that moment holds a special place in my heart to this day.

The Heart of the Family

We were a typical American family with wonderful busy years filled with baseball, basketball, flag football, music programs, Sunday school programs, Bible school, and fun family adventures. We spent a lot of time with the Brouwer family across the section. The Brouwer's place was our boys' second home since Mary helped take care of the boys when they were younger. Between their four kids and our three boys a lifetime bond was created. Our families often worked together baling hay. Of course when it came to putting that hay up in the barn, the boys, Mike, Carl, Brad, and Mark, had the task of sweating it out while stacking the hay in the haymow. Our boys quickly learned that on the farm the whole family works together mowing the lawn, feeding the sheep, taking care of the dogs, and weeding the garden. It wasn't long before the boys began walking the paper routes in town for spending money. In fact, the summer after Mark's eighth grade year, while he was on his paper route, he spotted his dream car, a 1972 Monte Carlo. He used those hard-earned paper route dollars to make the dream a reality. My husband, Dave, still has it in his heart to fulfill Mark's vision of restoring this car to its former glory.

Next to God, the importance of family always falls next in line for us. One of the most important steps Dave and I made early on in our marriage was the decision to worship in church together as a family. I grew up in the Catholic church, which taught me so much about discipline and obedience to God. However, the children's ministry in my husband's church spoke to my heart. After much prayer and consideration I became a member of that church and our family worshiped there together.

Dave and I also joined the new adult Sunday school class for young married couples. This class was being taught by Ed Thomas, the coach that introduced us in high school. What an interesting dynamic as Dave and I were, in a sense, back in "school" again. Dave, like many, still called him Coach. A bond was built and this became the beginning of our Christian walk, which my husband and I still share today.

Our class was challenged with questions about how we would respond to certain experiences in life. Many times these discussions would conclude with the realization that none of us ever know how we will respond when faced with trials in life, but that through our unwavering faith and belief, God would give us the strength to contend with whatever came our way. I still remember specific moments from those classes that give me such peace and strength.

What came next for our family was a myriad of highs and lows once Mark reached high school.

2

BOYS TO MEN

I t was May of Mark's eighth grade year, when we were driving to the "mandatory" spring meeting that Coach Thomas had "invited" all football players and their parents to, that it hit me: Mark is going to be in high school. Dave was particularly fond of these meetings since he was one of the football captains on Coach Thomas's first team at Parkersburg High School. As I sat and listened to Coach talking to his players and to all of the parents, I couldn't help but sense the excitement of the upcoming season. This inspirational meeting was intended to spur the players on for their summer physical and mental conditioning. The parents were then dismissed and Coach continued the meeting with just the players, challenging them to conduct themselves as gentleman, both on and off the field. Mark came away from the meeting with a playbook—which he better have studied by August—and a packet full of motivational and inspirational quotes and stories.

We hardly saw Mark that summer as he began a serious workout program with some of the guys in his class that included lifting weights and running to get in shape for football. These guys were so pumped about playing high school football. The time had finally come. They would finally be part of the football tradition they had admired and aspired to since their flag football days. The testosterone was plentiful amongst these would-be freshmen . . . and they thought life was pretty good!

When the season finally arrived, we were ready. Monday nights at the dinner table were spent with Mark and his dad discussing the scout report for the upcoming game. (Yes, Dave still played football through his boys. Come on, guys, don't tell me you don't do the same thing!) We joined the other parents, following our boys to football games all over the district. I still get pumped thinking about football game day! What a thrill watching your son running down on kickoffs and orchestrating the tackle just as the receiver catches the ball. As a linebacker, Mark was able to get in on a lot of the tackle action. All through the years, I never got tired of hearing the announcer calling, "Tackle made by Mark Becker" and Coach Thomas bellowing, "Way to go, Becker!" Yes, Coach also yelled if Mark did something wrong out there on the field. Dave and I, having been involved with sports ourselves, would often explain to all of our sons that if Coach quit yelling at you that means he's given up on you. Speaking of yelling, I don't think anyone wanted to sit by me at the games. I *encouraged* not only my boys but the whole team. Let's just say I got quite a workout at the games jumping up and down and hollering all night long. I get excited just thinking about it!

It would be remiss of me to refer to beautiful, crisp fall nights for all of these games. More likely than not, we experienced games when it was hot, humid, and the mosquitoes were biting us. There were also the games when it rained and we all huddled together on the bleachers to share umbrellas and vinyl ponchos. A good share of these young men were playing or dressing for games three nights a week. And yes, we attended every single game. It was a crazy, busy time but I loved being a football mom.

To teach them responsibility, Dave and I encouraged Brad and Mark to work for their own spending money, but I did hate the grueling routine that ensued. They both picked up jobs at our local grocery store. Before the normal school schedule of morning weight lifting and practices, Brad and Mark had to drag out of bed by 4:30 a.m. to drive eight miles to town to unload the truck at the local grocery store. They were troopers though and also worked many weekends, oftentimes until 10:00 p.m.

From One Season to Another

Mark sat down with Dave and me one night and said he wanted to give wrestling a try. "Mark, why do you want to do that? You're a good basketball player." I had been a basketball player so, of course, I wanted him to play basketball.

When he told us he would have to drop weight for the bracket he wanted to wrestle at, all kinds of red flags came up in my mind. I was concerned about Mark cutting weight during these important developmental years.

Well, Mark followed his dad's footsteps and it wasn't long before we were off to the gym to follow the wrestling meets. I have to admit wrestling is an exciting sport to watch as well. As the wrestling season labored on during those long, cold winter months, I noticed Mark started hanging out with some upperclassmen on the wrestling team. To the outward eye everything appeared okay.

One day between wrestling and track season, Mark came home, went to his bedroom, and lay on his bed. I sat on the bed beside him. Mark appeared to be struggling with something deep. He looked extremely tired and was on the verge of tears. "Mark, what's wrong?" I asked.

He just responded, "Nothing."

I could tell it wasn't "nothing" but Mark wouldn't let go of whatever was haunting him. I hugged him tight and reassured him he could talk to me about anything at any time.

We trusted Mark and he had never given us any reason not to trust him. However, a big changing point took place when Mark obtained his driver's license. Dave, Scott, and I were enjoying the weekend with my parents and family at

Clear Lake. Brad and Mark were both working at the grocery store that weekend. Saturday night I called Mark but he didn't answer his phone. I called Brad and he had no idea where Mark was. "Give me a call when he gets home, okay?" My gut started to knot up when Mark did not make it home that night. This was the first of many long, sleepless nights as I lay awake wracked with concerns about Mark.

Dave and I woke up early the next morning and headed for home. When Mark eventually walked through the door, I looked at him and he acted like nothing was out of the ordinary. "Where have you been and why didn't you answer your phone?" His facetious response was, "Hey, I was just camping and sitting by the campfire at Dean's pond." Dean is not his real name.

This guy was a few years older than Mark. But more importantly, Mark had not asked permission or even talked to us about this camping outing. This was so out of character for Mark. He knew the ground rules and deliberately disobeyed them. His actions did bring repercussions: Over the next few weeks Mark spent quality time at home with Mom, Dad, and Scott.

As Mark's high school years continued, we watched another side of Mark start to emerge. I couldn't understand why Mark was so quiet and seemed depressed. "Mark, why don't you get together with your friends from your class?"

"Mom, by the time I get off work at night, my classmates have already made their plans and are out of town. Besides, when I'm with the whole gang it feels like too many people and so much noise . . . it's just too loud."

Mark began to struggle with normal high school questions like, "Who are my friends?" "What is right and wrong?" and "Who am I?"

As parents, we read about what signs to look for with regard to drug use in our kids. However, we still weren't prepared for the phone call we received shortly after Mark's sixteenth birthday from our local sheriff. "Joan, I've got Mark here at the station. Could you and Dave come pick him up?" Arriving at the station, we sat down and found out the details of the night. Mark admitted to his dad and me that he was occasionally using marijuana. We were shocked, angry, and devastated by this news. I think what disturbed me even more was the question, "What is so terrible in life that Mark would even think about turning to marijuana?"

It was a quiet trip to town the next day when Mark, Dave, and I met with Coach Thomas and Mark confessed to Coach what he had been doing. Although he was beyond disappointed, Coach was supportive of Mark. Mark seemed relieved to clear the air and get this load off his chest. In addition to sitting out the required quarters of football for breaking the discipline policy, Mark also attended a substance abuse program.

As I drove Mark to those weekly meetings, it gave Mark and me a chance to talk about life. It was like the dam had finally broken. Mark shared so much of the confusion and fear he was experiencing. I have to admit I was quite discouraged one night as I waited in the parking lot for Mark to come out of his meeting. The guys in the car next to me were rolling a joint. I couldn't believe it! I began to doubt whether this program was really going to benefit Mark.

Coach Thomas had a lot of compassion for Mark and we were relieved when Coach helped Mark connect with a couple guys that were a year older than Mark. These guys were more on the quiet side and Mark seemed to mesh well with them and they became good friends.

One day Mark shared with me, "Mom, I've been saving up money and I'd like to buy a guitar. Can you go with me?" I was all over that. It excited me that Mark was taking an interest in something like music. Mark bought a wine-red Epiphone Les Paul Junior model guitar for a hundred bucks. Dave and I sweetened the deal by adding a 5-watt Marshall amplifier and some guitar lessons. A dream became reality for Mark that day. He and some friends started playing guitar together and even performed a few numbers at prom that year. Mark's love of playing guitar was born and this was the first of many guitars he purchased over the years.

Not Again

One summer night Brad called, "Mom, I just passed Mark in town and a cop has him pulled over." Mark had been stopped because his passenger had lit a firecracker and threw it out the window. Mark had drug paraphernalia in his car. *Lord, where is this coming from? Why, oh why can't our son see that this behavior leads to a dead end?* This time, since it was Mark's second infraction of the extracurricular disciplinary policy, Mark had to sit out even more football game quarters. Despite all of this, Mark's coaches told us he was one of the hardest working players on the team. Mark had more than disappointed his peers and coaches, and he appeared to be trying to earn their respect back.

Mark was required to meet with a probation officer and a substance-abuse counselor. He was eighteen now so everything was kept private between him and his counselor, but we saw Mark make huge strides in the right direction his senior year. His counselor helped him set personal goals and we could see Mark's self-esteem rise as he attained these goals.

Mark also started dating a really sweet gal so he had a friend to talk to and hang out with. Everyone needs someone *safe* to be around who doesn't judge them for their past and that girlfriend filled that ticket for Mark.

Later that next spring, when Mark and Dave joined other men from our church on a mission trip to a youth ranch in Arkansas, I was beyond excited. I prayed that this would be a profound trip for Mark, and from the stories he shared when he got back home, it sounded like this was an eye-opening experience for him. He told me he really appreciated his family and home life after meeting kids at the ranch who did not have homes or family support. This ranch was their chance to learn what life could be when given the love, support, and skills to survive.

As Mark graduated high school that spring, it appeared he was ready for the future. Or so we thought.

A Mother's Reflection

When someone is already struggling for reasons we do not yet know, the labels we all choose to place on that person tend to knock them down when they are already on their knees. Where was my faith at this time? I tried to give it over to God, but my humanness kept getting in the way of peace in this situation.

So much of what has happened in Mark's life is extremely difficult to revisit. During this time, I began to write in a journal. I didn't write every day. I didn't even write every month. I wrote when it was too painful to talk. I wrote when my tears clouded my mind and my total being with such sorrow that I couldn't even think straight. I wrote when sleep would not come. I wrote when I wondered where Mark was late at night.

It was a balmy spring night in May of Mark's senior year of high school. After some particularly long nights worrying about Mark, I made this entry in my journal:

Friday night we got a call from Mark that he was running late but not to worry and that he would be home soon. He got home about 1:30 a.m. and Dave and I were up so we could talk to him. What he had to say to us was very good. He spent Friday night with three other guys just talking about "stuff." These guys have had similar challenges like Mark has gone through and one of the boys doesn't get to play football his senior year at all because he has "messed up" three times! This particular guy has been very depressed the last few weeks and Mark decided to make him talk about it.

To make a long story short, Mark spent the evening telling these guys about God's love for all of us, even though we are sinners. He told them about God's forgiveness for all of our sins and tried to explain to them that they have to look ahead and try to find what God's plan is for their life.

Mark told us he didn't know where the words were coming from when he talked, but that it was the biggest "high" of his life Friday night!

Mark went on to say how sorry he was for everything he had put us through over the past years. He said that although he accepted God in his heart several years ago, he was just realizing what it was all about.

Wow! I've been waiting to hear this from Mark for a long time . . . needless to say, I didn't sleep the rest of the night. Praise God for this glimpse of awareness from Mark. We are not so naïve as to think Mark will never experience any more problems in making decisions and choices in his life; however, he is starting to "get it"!

Lord, please keep Mark protected from Satan. Protect him, Lord.

I went to bed that night thinking the worst was over and that Mark was ready to begin a new and better chapter in his life.

3

ONE STEP FORWARD, TWO STEPS BACK

Dave and I are strong proponents of getting a college degree and Mark, like most seniors, was struggling with the decision of where to attend college, or even if he wanted to attend college. Although we both attained associate degrees, we encouraged our boys toward a bachelor's degree, thinking it would give them an advantage in the working world.

Mark narrowed the search down to a four-year private college or a local community college, both colleges within thirty-five miles from where we lived. One day, Dave got out his old letters from college coaches and sat down with Mark.

"Mark, read these letters. I had the chance to go and play football at college but my mom and dad didn't support me or encourage me to do that. To this day I regret not at least giving college football a try." He then asked Mark, "Do you have any desire at all to try and play football at the college level?"

After weighing out the pros and cons of both college options, Mark did choose to attend Wartburg College and give football a try. He spent the summer mowing at our local golf course and continued his weight lifting and workout routine in preparation for college and the football program.

A few days before he was to begin college football, Mark said, "Mom, I think I should just go to Hawkeye Tech and work on my Gen Eds."

"Mark, this is too late to be making last-minute changes. We've completed all of the orientation, the registration, housing arrangements, and financial aid." I thought I was doing the right thing by encouraging Mark to stick with his original decision to go to Wartburg.

Moving Mark to college was an exciting day. Dave had built him an awesome loft bed for his dorm room. While he put that together, I helped Mark organize the rest of his belongings. At first Mark did well at college and we enjoyed following his football games. However, toward the end of the football season we started getting phone calls from Mark saying he didn't want to stay in school, he couldn't keep up with classes, and he sounded so incredibly sad. Mark was despondent when I tried to encourage him to move home and drive back and forth to classes. My mother's instinct was telling me that Mark didn't want to move back home because that would make him feel like he had failed but I could see Mark was suffering. He was quiet, withdrawn, and had an overall sad demeanor about him.

Mark did finish the semester and made the decision to transfer to the local community college. One night over Christmas break, Mark was excited to get together with a bunch of his former high school classmates at a party in a college town twenty miles away. We got a phone call that night, "Mom, I got arrested because I refused to take a breath test."

I responded, "What, did you get pulled over?"

"Yeah, I had a couple beers and was pulled over by the police when I left the party because a taillight was out on my car."

I told Mark, "Take the breath test so you don't have any more repercussions from this traffic stop."

Mark refused to take the sobriety test so that meant an automatic loss of his license for a year.

Here we go again, I thought. One step forward, two steps back.

Dave and I spent the night deliberating what Mark would do now that he didn't have a driver's license. How would he drive to school? How would he get a job? The next morning we picked him up and drove him to his apartment. "Mark, we have an option we want to discuss with you. Aunt Jane and Uncle Lu have offered you a job at their grocery store." We continued to discuss the pros and cons of him staying in the area or moving away and starting something new. Mark made the decision to move to northwest Iowa and begin working for his aunt and uncle.

Not My Son

It was while Mark was living with my sister and her husband, that my twin sister called me one day and said, "Joan, do you think Mark could have paranoid schizophrenia?" She had been observing Mark and researching behaviors she was seeing in him. She said when she talked to him it was like he didn't hear her. It was like he was focused on something else. Then, after a bit, he would respond to her question.

At the time, I did not even want to hear my sister suggest such an illness because I knew this was something I couldn't fix and for which there is no known cure. We continued to see our son struggling within himself and felt helpless as to what direction to turn to get him help.

Although Mark was beginning to make friends in northwest Iowa, the following summer Mark made the journey back to live in a city near our home. He moved in with a couple high school friends. It didn't take long before he got a job in landscaping, which he really enjoyed.

That fall was a rough time in my life. I had begun traveling throughout Iowa for my work. On a Sunday morning in October, I awoke to my husband talking gibberish and flailing his hand toward me. I became alarmed when he couldn't talk, and I asked him what was wrong. I finally made out that he was trying to say 9-1-1. I made the call and started praying. After a couple days of tests, the doctors suggested that Dave had a TIA (transient ischemic attack). This, along with travel, keeping up with my youngest son Scott's school schedule, and Mark's up-and-down lifestyle, had me at my wit's end.

A couple days after Dave had his medical attack, Mark called. "Mom, is dad okay? I heard he died." I told him, "No, Mark, your dad had a scare but he is okay. I tried to reach you but you wouldn't answer your phone." Mark went on to tell me he didn't want to continue to live this way and asked us for help. We arrived to pick him up and took him to the hospital. Once again, Mark had succumbed to the battle of using drugs. We didn't understand why he kept turning to this behavior. Mark had not been taking care of himself and at the hospital we learned he had bronchitis and a bacterial infection. He kept saying over and over again, "I'm so sorry. I just want to spend time with you and dad and my brothers."

Mark moved back home with us and picked up some odd jobs here and there. This was a time when Mark healed physically, emotionally, and spiritually. I was still concerned about how quiet Mark was though. Mark was living in his own world and didn't invite us in to share it with him. Why wouldn't he open up to us about it?

A Fresh Start, Again

It was a beautiful fall day when we were, again, helping Mark move back to the Cedar Valley area about thirty miles from home. He had acquired a job at a grocery store and decided to go to a local community college to study landscaping. He made arrangements to move in with some gals he had gone to high school with. As was becoming a well-trod pattern with Mark, at first he did really well at school and work. He seemed happy to have some purpose and independence. However, when I visited Mark, I could still see the battle he was having with, what I continued to think, was depression.

That spring one of Mark's roommates called and said, "Joan, we are really worried about Mark. He just sits on the couch day after day and he won't leave the house. I'm sorry, but we don't want to be responsible for him. Can you please come and get him?"

Once again, Dave and I went to pack up Mark's belongings and move him home. Mark admitted to us that he had again started using some drugs and that he didn't want to continue on with this kind of life.

When Mark moved home we could see drugs were not the real battle. He quit taking them seemingly without any problems or side effects whatsoever. There was more to it. We could see it, we could sense it, and we just didn't know what to do about it.

Dave, Mark, and I made a visit to our local medical clinic's staff psychologist. Even though Mark did not continue to see that doctor, he agreed to see the medical doctor that had attended him from the time he was born. Mark needed to try and get to the bottom of why he kept trying to escape life, why he kept running away from reality. Why, why, why? Mark started taking some medication at this time, and it seemed to help him sleep better at night and helped keep at bay the demons that tormented him.

Here are some notes from my journal after a particularly difficult night with Mark when he had gone out and he called us for help. He was scared for his life.

Last night Mark called us . . . we went and picked him up. The anguish and pain I see in my son's face, heart, and entire being fills me with sadness. He struggled so to hold everything in. I know he is hurting terribly, but he doesn't want to talk. It's as if he was rewinding his entire life before us . . . like a record and bleeps of things coming out.

- I'm sunk either way.
- I just want to find a nice girl, get married, and have a family.
- Why am I like this?
- I wish I knew what is wrong with me.
- I want to save money and remove this thing (pointing to the tattoo on his back).
- I'm dyslexic . . . I can't read, I can't type.
- I can beat this by myself, right?
- I might have to go away for a while.
- Drugs are the devil . . . I didn't know they would do this to me.

  I'm straight, right, Mom? I'm okay, right?

Dave and I just sat and listened, held him tight, prayed with him . . . Dave slept downstairs by Mark. Mark is absolutely terrified . . . I don't know if it is drugs making him feel this way or what?

I sense he is in some type of trouble . . . serious trouble from past choices and actions . . . and scared.

Lord, you know Mark's hurts, fears . . . everything about him. We know that only you, God, can perform a miracle with Mark and take away *all* desire for drugs and sinful ways. I beseech, thee, Lord to come and whisk away my son to safety. Show Dave and me the way to help . . . you know our inadequacies . . . you know we've tried everything we know how to do . . . we know it's not in our power, but only in your power, mercy, and grace. Mark needs professional help . . . God would you show us and point us to someone . . . a Christian man or woman . . . who, by your grace, can help Mark?

I'm scared too, Lord. I've prayed for you to work in Mark's life . . . to do *anything* it takes to get his attention. When I pray that prayer I have to be prepared for *anything* as well.

We've watched and lived Mark's struggles for over four years now, Lord. I know everything is

in your time, Lord . . . I do pray for strength to
get through today . . . just one day at a time.

I love you, Lord, and I do believe ALL things
are possible through you.

Matthew 4:10–11: "Jesus said to him, 'Away
from me, Satan! For it is written; Worship the Lord
your God, and serve him only.' Then the devil left
him, and the angels came and attended him."

Lord, keep the angels attending Mark,
please?

Even after Mark moved back home and even though he
was trying so hard to be "normal," I have to admit I didn't
trust him. I felt horrible about not trusting him. I just wished
Mark would open up and actually *talk* to us and tell us what
was going on in that head of his. Maybe that's what he was
trying to do in this letter he wrote to me on Mother's Day
that year:

Mom,

I read the letter you wrote this morning,
and I just have got to say that, it feels like you
and I might communicate our feelings or just
regular priorities differently. If it caused you
to write from your heart and made you feel so
"lied to" by me I gotta let you know where I am

coming from these days. Honestly, I don't want you to misunderstand me right now, please. I apologize for the late night, a lot on mind the last few weeks and last night. You and Dad included! Not to forget Scott and Brad but they seem to be doing just fine for themselves unless I'm missing something.

Can you see that I'm living a life that broke its previous mold or "walk" and still can improve for me and my family because I love you guys so much? It is hard for me to hear and think about you losing sleep because of me. Why? I lose sleep for reasons I don't even know but not because I lost some control on someone's (my) life schedule. I don't always come across the best way, or on time—I know—but who's perfect?

Someday I hope I can really understand your views or opinion on parenting a twenty-one-year-old that's just doing what he can. But it never seems to be enough for his boss, family, friends, anyone he talks to anymore; plus himself more and more! The times he (I) falls short of his closest friends (you and dad), it's a shot to an entire twenty-one-year-old's personal confidence. You say I'm vulnerable but how much more do you want me to be? I am vulnerable because I want to be like someone else. You and Dad are great role models and very knowledgeable on just about any issue. But I can't stand it when you won't come to terms with me being an *individual*.

Mom, right now I'm growing in healthy ways that will last and be worthwhile to our family more and more every day. My number one lifetime goal is positively to leave a lasting or an upright mark or memory. Might not make sense now. It has been hard but I think it has been rubbing off the wrong way lately. If you could understand how grateful and proud I feel about this home of ours, I don't think you'd worry about me living a life that is of God's respect or way.

I have livable dreams that won't just be walked out with everyday ease but with care and value in minds. Life is about change. Goals and dreams ought to accompany life's path fluidly, whichever new or old way is thrown at ya. Make any sense? Just know that your second son is not lost or as "out there" as he seems, trust me. You know what I want? It is to be like Joan, Dave, Brad, and Scott! I cannot help it that the road you all walk is an original/ good and *true* road; Or that it has just been brought to my eyes! Just in time because that

old path was just too wearing and unfulfilling.
I think that sometimes, when ya think ur doing
it right, it might be a rationalization for that
person's comfort. I understand that I was lost in
my selfish, childish procrastinations. Not a good
combination obviously.

Family. You repeatedly threw me life
preservers. I was selfish. Your love and beautiful
smiles of assurance and happiness are all I need
and rely on. Especially when somebody looks at
or on to me for help/words in the middle of my
confusion. Those smiles and your presence in
my life boosts my confidence. My confidence is
funny. That thinking that gets so high, so low,
overfilled to depleted over periods of time when
I didn't realize what matters. It's not perfect
for anyone I don't think, I'm still finding that
balanced center that doesn't leave me when I
need it.

I gotta say I feel like we've gotten a lot closer
in the last few months. Or not, I dunno? I'm just
going to say I'm different and not ashamed to
be myself. Different because God's light changed
me. Thankfully I saw it and he was forgiving
enough, and to be so awesome at a time
when nothing else seemed to be alive at the
time. It has blown me away from the chemical

dependency. It became the first thought, the crutch or way of thinking when I used to get up every morning. No joke. Now I move free of that, on my own with God to thank.

Last, thanks for exposing me to God's free gifts to us when I was young. That was a good seed for sure. His everlasting, all-surrounding love that can be thought of as "over-the-top" sometimes because it never ceases. I know he is in your heart, Mom, because you always love like that for some reason. In my old and new eyes you are smart, graceful, and beautiful, and your love is strong—always has been.

Mark Daryl Becker

Dave and I confided in Brad and brought him up to speed with Mark's situation. Brad, about to graduate from Iowa State University, invited Mark to come and live with him in South Dakota. Mark readily agreed this would be a fresh, new start. I was still concerned about Mark's health. Depression didn't quite seem the right fit, and we knew Mark was not using any drugs, but something wasn't right. My mother's gut was telling me there was something wrong, and I just did not know what to do about it. I prayed that God would reveal whatever it was that Mark needed to cure him.

When Mark moved in with his brother in South Dakota he began working at a distribution center. We visited Brad and Mark often. It appeared like it was a good move for Mark but I still had this uneasy feeling that Mark was struggling with something beyond his grasp. I tried to convince Mark to see a counselor to discuss how he was feeling but he resisted. During one of our visits he said, "Mom, I've had a lot of time to think about my past. I can see now that people pretended to be my friends but they were just using me. I hate to go to sleep at night because I hear voices." He went on to explain to me why, when he was little, he would want to sleep with Dave and me. He said it was because he has fought these voices as far back as he can remember. He talked a lot about angels protecting him. He said, "Mom, remember when I came back home and would be looking out the window during the night? There are these frightening, dark images, but they slink away from God's angels."

This explained to me why many times, as a child, in the middle of the night Mark would clamber over me in bed to secure himself between his dad and me. We welcomed his company and hugged him tight to bring him the rest he sought. One particular night Dave woke up to noises out in the living room—sort of a scurrying sound. Dave cautiously went to investigate only to see Mark darting across the floor from one chair to another, trying to hide. We didn't think too much of this, assuming it was sleepwalking. We just tucked Mark back into bed and fell back into bed ourselves. Now it made sense as Mark explained the absolute terror he felt each night, alone in his room.

After a few months in South Dakota, Mark moved on to a new job and started working in the bakery department at a local grocery store. He said he loved making bread. I was so happy for him and continued to pray God would protect him.

Here are notes from my journal after Mark moved to South Dakota:

One year ago . . . Lord . . . one year ago our son didn't want to live the life he had been living any more. You know what his exact thoughts were and you knew his sins but You gave him life . . . hope . . . you saved him, Lord.

I will never forget the miracle you performed in Mark's life. I praise you!

Now . . . I seek your wisdom in how that whole experience can be used for your glory. Not only do I believe you will use Mark in a powerful way, but I want to be your humble servant and have you use me in some way.

I want to share with others about your saving grace and miraculous deeds and about the peace, comfort, and strength you gave our family throughout this time.

You know the anguish we felt when Dave and I knew we couldn't help our son in our power . . . we knew that only you, Lord, could save our son and give him life. Please show me the way, Lord, give me the words, Lord, and give me the strength, Lord, to share the love you have given me with others.

Thank you for your blessings, thank you for the hard times, thank you for the good times . . . use me Lord in whatever way you need me! I am completely yours, Lord.

Thinking back over the past several years, I realized we had weathered many storms along the way. I took comfort in knowing God has been with us every step of the way. I was feeling pretty confident things were looking up, finally. What I didn't realize at the time was that the storms had just begun.

4

THE EF5 TORNADO

May 25, 2008, began like many Memorial Day weekends as Dave and I enjoyed a leisurely drive to my parents' home at the lake. After lunch, we all sat around the patio table drowsily watching the water as it ebbed and flowed. The gentle breeze became a strong wind that was switching like a polka of sorts; one-two-three (hop), one-two-three (hop), and the sky began to turn ominously dark in the south. My stomach started churning as we hurried inside to turn on the television and check out the weather. As we followed the track of the storm, we were mesmerized by the orange, red, and purple rotations appearing on the radar. I turned to Dave and uttered, "We are going home right now!"

On the drive home our car felt like a turtle creeping along at incredibly slow speeds as we wanted to rush to get there, but Dave tried to keep his speed close to the limit. My phone rang, and I heard my oldest son say, "Mom, this is Brad. I just heard a tornado hit Parkersburg and that a good part of the town is gone, including the school." We couldn't believe it . . . We didn't believe it!

I reminded him, "You know how exaggerated these stories can get. We're on our way now. We'll keep you posted." However, as emergency vehicles from every community north of Parkersburg started to whiz by us, I remember starting to shake with fear and premonition that perhaps this time it wasn't an overstatement of the facts.

We made a quick stop at home to throw on old clothes and pick up supplies—flashlights, chain saws, and whatever else Dave could think of in about a two-minute time span—and sped the remaining eight miles into town. Dave worked for the county and was part of the response team for emergencies such as this. We weren't prepared for what slapped us in the face when we arrived in Parkersburg. It was like a war zone. People were staggering in shock, many barefooted, many bleeding. It was pouring rain.

We began to navigate through the downed trees, power lines, people, debris from cars, houses, and buildings. At one point, I just stepped on the brakes and stopped the truck. I was frozen and couldn't move. Dave told me later he was yelling for me to drive but I couldn't even hear him. Nothing was familiar and our landmarks were gone, but we eventually made it to where the emergency teams were setting up. I remember seeing Coach Thomas watching his wife, Jan, as she helped organize the emergency responders. I went and asked Coach how he was and how his house fared? He flatly said,

"It's gone, Joan, everything is gone." I gave him a hug and said, "You and Jan are here, Ed. Let's be thankful for that."

Dave instinctively grabbed his chain saw and joined other Parkersburg natives in sawing up the trees clogging the streets. As I attempted to move our truck, I was flagged down and asked to get town maps printed for the emergency personnel. Since the highways were jammed with cars, I figured the quickest option would be to drive four miles west down a gravel road to the Middle School in Aplington. Somehow I managed to keep the pickup under control as I rushed to get those maps printed and delivered back to Parkersburg.

It was getting dark and the town was under a mandatory evacuation. Dave and I both stumbled around with flashlights trying to find each other. In our panic we didn't know that our cell phones wouldn't work since all communications were shut down except for emergency frequencies. Eventually, we found our way back to each other. As we headed home, emergency personnel flagged us down and asked if we could help. As these first responders conducted house-to-house searches, they found an elderly lady just sitting in the dark in her home. She was in shock and it took quite a few questions before we were able to ascertain that she did have family we could contact. When we finally got her delivered safely into the arms of her family, our pickup got us home that night as if on autopilot. Our minds were reeling from the scene in town. We were some of the fortunate ones. We had a bed at home to sleep in that night. Who knew this devastation was only the beginning of what was yet to come in our lives and, subsequently, the people in our community's lives as well.

The EF5 Aftermath

The morning after the tornado hit, Dave, our son Scott, and I maneuvered our way into town to begin helping clean up the debris. After our third attempt to find an open route into town and miles of driving highways and gravel roads, we finally found the point of entry to take us through security to enter the remnants of our town. Our first destination took us to my brother-in-law's mother's house—or where her house used to be—to help her search for valuables. There was no home left, just part of the basement and rubble. I'll never forget the picture that haunts me: seeing Sylvia sitting in a lawn chair in the middle of where her house used to stand, just watching in bewilderment as family and friends sifted through the shambles of glass, splintered wood, twisted aluminum siding, and soggy drywall. I'm not sure any of us even knew what to look for, just that we needed to do *something . . . anything* to make us think we were helping in some tangible way.

Next we headed to the football field. Dave and I stared at the mayhem and didn't know how to begin the seemingly impossible task of cleaning up the debris. As we deliberated with Coach Thomas, he put his arm around Dave's shoulders and asked, "Dave, do you think you can help get this mess cleaned up so we can play football this fall?" Coach's goal was to play football at the field in Parkersburg by fall. He felt that if our community could look forward to something "normal" like football, it would go a long way in healing the hearts and minds of the hundreds of people dealing with the shock of losing their homes, some even losing their beloved family members. Without knowing how, Dave responded, "Sure will Coach."

Dave lay awake that night praying for answers of where to start with this monumental task before him. It's amazing how God responds to our prayers. The next day at the county shop where Dave is the equipment superintendent, he received a phone call from a contractor in north-central Iowa. "Hey, we own some trucks and wanted to see how we could help with the tornado cleanup. I decided to call the county's shop to see if you could give us some direction." Boy, could Dave give them some direction! After providing the contractor with the details of where to register as volunteers, he set up the time for them to come and start picking up scrap metal. Dave proceeded to enlist the help of a good friend of ours, Jim Clark. These guys spearheaded getting all of the mangled fencing and bleachers removed from the football field, practice field, softball diamond, and baseball field so contractors could begin rebuilding. Not only did this trucking contractor volunteer his people, equipment, and fuel, he also sent the checks for the scrap metal proceeds to the school. What an awesome example of how the entire Midwest joined together to help our community rebuild from this disaster!

The summer of 2008 became a foggy blur to me, and probably to everyone else in our community. A pattern began of working our jobs during the day, heading to the football field to work until after dark, and then taking our hurting, filthy, dirty selves back home for a few hours of sleep. The physical work I was involved in brought to the forefront muscles I didn't even know I had. Weekends became round-the-clock work at the field, organizing volunteers, picking up debris, and continuing the all-out effort to get the field cleaned up and ready to go, but always allowing ourselves fellowship and rest at church on Sunday morning.

One night at dusk as the cool of the summer evening was starting to descend, Dave and I were surveying the work that had been completed and the work that was yet to be done still. Coach Thomas walked up to Dave and me and explained some football teams were coming to help with the tornado cleanup the next day and wondered what they could do. I said, "Well, Coach, it may not seem too glamorous, but this football field needs someone to get on their hands and knees and dig out every shard of glass." The next day the local news showed those volunteer football players on their hands and knees with five-gallon buckets doing exactly that task.

A Call Out of Nowhere

One evening, I took time out to drive the fifty-mile round trip to stock up on much-needed food and supplies. As I was walking down the aisle of the store, my phone rang. It was Mark calling. I could hardly hear him as he whispered, "Mom, I'm okay. Quit worrying about me. I know you are trying to get into my head, but I'm okay." I had my mind so focused on finding the next item on my grocery list that I asked Mark to repeat what he just said.

When he did, I told him, "I know you're okay, Mark. What in the world are you talking about?" I chatted with Mark a few minutes and caught him up with our cleanup work in town. I was so sidetracked on the busyness of what was going on that Mark's bizarre conversation didn't immediately register.

However, when Brad called a few days later he sounded worried. He told me, "Mom, something is going on with Mark, and I don't know what to do. I'm never quite sure what to expect when I come home from work." Brad proceeded to explain that some days when he walked in the door after work Mark seemed just fine. But that on other days he was like an entirely different person. "I walk in the door and he's yelling and trying to start a physical fight with me . . . just out of nowhere. Mom, I don't know who this person is."

As the disturbing, strange calls from Mark continued, I started to get very concerned. Even though I was exhausted from work and the crazy schedule we were keeping, I told

Dave I was going to squeeze in the four-and-a-half-hour
trip to South Dakota to see for myself what was going on.
Thursday night, just as I was packing my bag, Mark called me
and said, "Mom, I want to move back home. I want to be able
to watch Scott play football and be a part of his life." Mark
had either quit his job or lost his job. I'm not sure which, but
he just wanted to come home.

Oh Lord, now what? Dave and I spent several hours that
night debating what we should do. We did not think it was
Brad's responsibility to be wrangling with Mark's situation,
so by 6:00 a.m. the next morning I was on the road to South
Dakota to move Mark home, yet again.

It was building up to a hot summer day as I pulled into
the driveway of the home our sons were sharing. Mark was
sitting on the front step waiting for me. His car was packed
to the brim with his most important possessions. No rest
for this mom. Since Brad was going to drive my car back to
Parkersburg when he got off work, Mark and I hopped in his
car and started the drive east toward home-sweet-home.

The atmosphere was uncomfortable in the car and Mark
was tense. I broke the silence by saying, "Mark, you know it
will not be easy to move back to the Parkersburg area. How
are you going to handle the way of life you left there?"

He told me he wasn't the same person he used to be and
that he would make sure he communicated that to everyone.
This conversation lasted all of fifteen minutes and we settled
into a deafening quiet. It wasn't long before we crossed the

South Dakota border into Iowa. At this point, Mark turned
to me and quietly said, "Can you feel it, Mom? Can you feel
it?" I was chilled as I turned to look at him and asked what
he was talking about. He sort of shook his head and said
he could just feel something strange coming over him. My
mind, my whole being, experienced a sense of foreboding.

5

IT'S ONLY JUST BEGUN

I was wrought with so many different emotions as Mark settled in and began setting up his living area in our walk-out basement that had lots of large windows.

Happiness—to have Mark back home.

Fear—that Mark would not be able to find a job.

Sadness—to see Mark trying to find his place in life.

Anger—at myself for my lack of faith and trust in Mark because of his past.

If I can't even let go of that history, how can I ever expect our community and others to give Mark another chance to prove himself and succeed?

Within a week Mark had a bounce in his step as he walked into the house one afternoon. "Mom, I'm going to start work next week for a place that builds custom cabinets for commercial clients like schools and offices."

"Oh, Mark, I am so thankful you have found a job that you can use your natural talents. I know how you like building things. What a great opportunity!" I gave him a hug as I expressed my pride in his success.

Mark commenced a daily routine of driving thirty-five miles to and from work. My job continued to take me throughout the state of Iowa each week. I was a bit jealous of the special bond that Dave and Mark began to build with each other, yet grateful Mark had a dad that loved him and could connect with him. At night, as they compared their workday stories, Mark began to absorb the Weber grilling technique from the grill master himself—his dad. The lazy summer nights would meld into a good eight-hour sleep only to be rudely awakened with the 5:30 a.m. alarm. Another workday would begin.

Frankly, I could almost forget about my concerns about Mark while living out of hotel rooms working long stressful hours at client sites. Each Friday, although I was excited about spending the weekend with my guys, the drive home gave me too much time to think about Mark and the doubts would begin to surface again. Even though Mark's move home appeared to be in order, deep down inside I had this sense that Mark was dealing with something completely different than I had ever observed before. Maybe it's because I only saw Mark on the weekends that I noticed him beginning to withdraw into himself. My lack of trust came to the forefront as I wondered if he was using marijuana but I was afraid to even confront him about it.

I believe Dave was trying to shield me, or perhaps he was just in denial. As we spent quiet nights on the deck catching up from the week, the truth would begin to emerge about Mark's strange behavior. Dave told me that some days Mark would come home from work and he seemed perfectly normal, but then in the next minute it was like he was in another world. We both noticed he seemed to be looking at something or someone that wasn't visible to us in the room. I would catch Mark talking to himself. He would laugh at something or someone that we couldn't hear or see. Dave and I would try to talk to Mark about it but it was like he didn't even hear us speaking to him. We were at a loss as to how to approach Mark about this bizarre behavior. I think the hardest part about all of this is that much of the time Mark appeared to be himself and it was just great to be with him. It was like Dave and I were treading on a delicate glass surface and we didn't want it to shatter.

From Strange to Psychotic

With apprehension I allow myself to think back to that September night of terror when we woke up to Mark yelling, "Get off me, get away from me, help me!" I shivered and wondered, *Is there an intruder in the house?* Dave was wary as he made his way downstairs and found Mark crouching a few feet away from his bed, fighting off something or someone Dave couldn't see. Mark implored his dad to protect him, "Don't you see them, Dad? Please, just help me! They're attacking me from everywhere! The walls, under the bed, the ceiling. I'm tired of him yelling and sending his goons after me."

I stood at the top of the steps too terrified to descend. I was shivering as I listened in horror to Mark's fears being unleashed. Who and what was he yelling about?

Somehow Dave broke through Mark's chaotic mind and convinced him to climb the stairs. Maybe if he could get him out of the basement Mark would calm down. Dave and I started to try to talk with Mark and explain that there was no one attacking him and we could not see anyone. How utterly ridiculous to think we could even begin to delve into a psychotic mind and reason with him. He accused us of working against him and started distorting our words and actions. Of course, now we realize there is no rationalizing with someone who is in the middle of a delusional attack but at that time we didn't know what to do or what to say during this bizarre event.

I was incredulous as Mark began to rant about people in our church and the Parkersburg community. "You're all part of a big conspiracy to get into the minds of the children in our town! You don't believe me, do you? Can't you see? Thomas is sending them to attack me! They're here right now. Maybe I better go to town and talk some sense into Ed, and you guys too." Dave and I couldn't believe what we were hearing. Mark had the utmost respect for Coach Thomas.

The more we tried to talk to Mark, the more it seemed to incite him. There were silent breaks and he would just stare at us and I would think, okay, we're done with this. Then he would start in again, "Dave and Joan, why won't you believe me?" As I tried to comfort him he said, "F_____ you, get away from me!" He kept brushing at his arms saying he had to get the feathers off. His skin felt clammy and cold, his face looked swollen, and his body language was exaggerated and vulgar. He was flailing his arms, grabbing himself, stomping around, and yelling all the while. This was behavior we had never experienced or observed in our son before that calamitous night.

Desperate, I went to my chair and started reading my Bible. I was stricken with an absolute feeling of helplessness. An inability to do anything! I had no idea where to turn, who to call for help, what to do. I started to read my Bible out loud and there were moments Mark would stop, listen, and stare at me. *Okay, Lord, maybe he is hearing this.* Unfortunately, it was just a short reprieve before he would start the tirade all over again.

Dave and I tried over and over to convince Mark to let us take him to the doctor and even attempted to get Mark into a car so we could take him to the emergency room at the hospital. Mark, in his psychotic state, was extremely strong and resistant to help of any kind. He considered his dad and me a threat.

After a couple of hours, at my wit's end, I quietly asked Mark to leave the house. Mark seemed to hear what I said.

At this point he flatly responded, "I guess I would be better off dead since you won't help me or believe what I say." He actually seemed to be coming back into his own mind as he dejectedly left the house around 5:00 a.m.

This was the first time we observed a full-blown psychotic episode experienced by our son. I was incredibly sad and afraid as I watched Mark leave. The exhaustion was setting in and we didn't have a clue where to turn for help. What if Mark was going to go off and have an accident or maybe even try to kill himself? Dave and I drank coffee, we prayed together aloud, and continued to wonder with each other what we should do. We talked about calling the sheriff to ask them what a person should do in this situation.

As was becoming customary, I turned to my journal to try and sort out my emotions in those wee hours. Here are my writings from the morning after Mark left the house:

> We've been up since 3:00 a.m. listening to him struggle with himself . . . it is like his mind is twisting every good thing into evil. Perhaps it is not drugs but a chemical imbalance. I actually feared what he would do to himself or to our family . . . I've never felt that way before.
>
> I asked him to leave about 5:00 a.m. He was yelling, hitting things, throwing things . . . saying some really awful stuff. I know it is not Mark talking, but the confused thoughts inside.

Lord, where do we go from here? I will never lose faith that you can perform miracles . . . but I also know that Mark has to walk/turn to you and not keep turning his back on you. I don't know what to do, where to turn, who to ask for help . . . Dave and I don't know where to turn . . . other than you, Lord. I'm so incredibly sad right now.

Midmorning we heard car tires crunching up the driveway. Mark was home and when he walked in the door we held our breaths hoping "our son" was back. No such luck . . . the horrific cycle started all over again. We implored Mark to let us take him to the hospital, and when he refused, I snuck back to my bedroom to call the local sheriff's department. After explaining Mark's bizarre behavior I asked for help. As I hung up the phone, Dave came to see how the phone conversation went. I relayed to him that the sheriff was on the way. The unspoken thoughts between us said it all . . . fear, defeat, vulnerability, sadness . . . the list goes on.

When the sheriff arrived he talked to Mark outside. I'm not sure exactly what Mark said, but eventually the sheriff came inside. Dave and I attempted to explain the horror of the night, what we had witnessed, what we had heard, and our overwhelming concern over Mark's statement about being "better off dead." The sheriff discussed the option of a mental health committal for evaluation. My head was throbbing and my eyes were swollen with the thousands of tears I had cried over the previous hours. I was numb as the sheriff began to explain that one of us would have to write a statement explaining why Mark should be committed. He continued on to say that he would write the second statement. The sheriff tried one more time to convince Mark to agree to go on his own to the hospital, but again, he was unsuccessful.

I went to the courthouse to fill out the committal statement. Within a few hours the sheriff arrived at our home to pick up Mark. Mark begged, he pleaded, "Please, don't let them take me away!" My heart was torn out of my chest at that point and Dave and I completely broke down. We had never felt so alone. Not only did we not fully understand the committal process, we didn't know who to reach out to that could answer our questions. What will happen to Mark at the hospital? Will Mark be restrained in a bed? Will he get to talk to a psychiatrist? When can *we* explain the details of Mark's episode and to whom? I felt so guilty for sending my son away, even though I didn't know what else could be done given the state he was in.

Dave and I sat at the table regurgitating the events. We decided to call Leo (not his real name) who was an acquaintance of ours from church. We knew he had prior experience working with young people and had studied demonic forces. After work he stopped by our house and we explained what we had experienced with Mark during the night. Leo asked us if Mark had taken any drugs. I told him that Mark had been home all night and that, no, we didn't see him take anything. I explained to him we had seen our son in prior years when he did use drugs. The behavior Mark displayed the prior night was something completely different than we had ever experienced. We asked Leo if he had ever encountered something like this and he appeared to be at a loss as well. Because of Mark's vulgar language and actions he had exhibited during the night I said, "It's like some other force has taken over his body. This is not our son saying those awful words! It's not the sound of his voice and his face didn't even look like his." As we talked and prayed, we discussed the possibility of this being a satanic attack.

Leo asked us to let him know when Mark got out of the hospital. He said he would be willing to spend time with Mark if Mark agreed to it.

I called the sheriff and found out Mark would be at the hospital for a week. I had complete confidence Mark would be meeting with professionals who were going to be able to get to the root of what was wrong with Mark. Each night we made the 120 mile round trip to visit Mark. Unfortunately, we quickly found out from conversing with Mark that hardly any of his time had been spent with a doctor or psychiatrist.

Here are some thoughts from my journal during that long, agonizing week of Mark's committal:

We've been going to see him every night and have had some really good conversations. Mark knows what he has to do . . . but I also know he needs help or medication to bring a balance to his system.

Lord, why do I feel so guilty about Mark being confined in a place that can help him? This is so heartbreaking . . .

Mark kept telling us the doctor had told him he didn't have to stay the entire week if we would rescind the committal papers. We actually did speak with the doctor for about five minutes one night and he said if Mark agreed to follow the doctor's release orders, Mark could go home.

Although I did follow through with the requested paper work, Mark was not released until the full week was up. Dave and I were naïve and ignorant about how this process was supposed to work and exactly what chain of events was to take place while Mark was at this hospital. To my uneducated mind, it appeared the hospital was just going through the motions and that they did not really care at all to try and delve into what was really going on in Mark's brain. Could we believe what Mark, in his condition, told us? Why didn't the doctors sit down with us and ask about Mark's medical history? Why didn't anyone ask us what had occurred in our home with our son? Why, if I was a part of the process that committed my son to this hospital, was I never asked the details of Mark's episode?

When your child is sick, your heart is filled with compassion for him. I don't care if that child is three or twenty-three. Every night as we made that dark trip to the hospital, Dave and I kept hashing over what we should have or should not have done. We were desperate to speak with someone who could help us understand. I was angry at our inadequacies regarding this situation and how helpless we felt.

During our visits, Mark would talk for a few minutes but then he wanted us to leave . . . So many unspoken words. I could see the struggle in his face as his thoughts took him to an unknown place. I wanted him to just spit it out, yell at us, anything! But perhaps that is exactly what he was trying to do that night of terror when he alternated between begging us for help and accusing us of conspiracy.

Here are notes from my journal during this time:

Although I had filled out a sheet dropping the petition I filed, the court somehow didn't get it processing to dismiss the case. We did pick up Mark (praise God)! Mark was very upset the judge pushed the hearing back for sixty days. I called the court when I got home because they had not given Mark a copy of the sheet I had filled out . . . I want Mark to see that I did follow through with what I said I would do . . . just as he followed through at Mason City.

On the other hand, why is Mark so upset about reporting back to the judge about seeing a counselor and taking his prescriptions? It is what he told us and the doctor at Mason City he would do anyway.

Lord, I love my son, and I have to let him live his life. I completely surrender all to you, Lord . . . take him, mold him, protect him, fill him.

I look forward to seeing the man he will become . . . because I know he loves you, Lord . . . and I know you are with him.

I'm done . . . I will journal no more . . . God, *you* are in control.

〰️

It was a long silent drive from the hospital to the courthouse. We had been given permission to pick Mark up from the hospital and take him to the courthouse for his hearing. I was upset that we were not allowed to go into the judge's chambers with Mark. I have mixed emotions about that day: being incredibly happy that Mark was out of the hospital but equally sad because Mark was so angry with us about the committal. His situation certainly did not improve when he refused to tell his employer why he was in the hospital for a week. That decision lost him his job.

It took a couple days, but Mark eventually started to talk to open up about how he was feeling and what bizarre thoughts, voices, and images were swirling around in his brain. I asked him if he had been taking any drugs prior to his psychotic episode and he said he had smoked some marijuana but that was all. He said he was trying to escape the voices but the marijuana didn't help . . . the voices continued.

Mark and I took a walk down our long driveway and I tried to explain to him my concerns about his health and what I had observed in him since he had moved home. In fact, I offered to let him read my journal from the prior years. I needed to share with Mark what my thoughts and emotions are when he is obviously suffering and the hopeless feeling I have when I can't help him. Mark agreed at this time to follow up with a counselor and take the medication prescribed. Unfortunately, when Mark went to pick up his prescription, there was a problem with the debit card the county case management system had given him. Mark became frustrated and embarrassed when the card wouldn't work.

When someone with a brain illness finally gets brave enough to take that enormous step toward purchasing their medication and they are faced with a situation like this, it can be devastating and even life altering. We did help Mark get that medication, but what a battle.

Dave and I were frustrated with "the system," since at this time we still did not know if there was a diagnosis. Are there side effects of the medication we should be aware of? Who is Mark going to be accountable to? And what was our role supposed to be in Mark's treatment?

I was angry . . . at Mark and with the committal; but mostly at myself for not understanding how the mental health system was supposed to work! This is where you need to begin not just knocking on doors to get answers, but you need to pound those doors down if you are *not* getting answers.

Ignorance is bliss. That's what they say anyway. Maybe that's a good thing, because little did we know, the psychotic episodes had only just begun for Mark.

6

HELP!
IS ANYONE LISTENING?

Over the next few months, although I hate to admit it, we became accustomed to Mark displaying strange behaviors of talking to people who were not there, staring into space, and not hearing a thing we were saying to him. At times it was like he was in an entirely different world, and yet at other times he was "our" Mark with that beautiful smile and wit about him.

The psychotic episodes continued but there was no set pattern, time, or consistency. Mark could literally be sitting with us at home and, at just a snap of a finger, go into one of his episodes. Some episodes were pretty mild, some were more extreme. Mark started sleeping upstairs on the couch and told us he was frightened of being attacked downstairs. It became a regular event for Dave and me to take turns sleeping in the living room near Mark. These were long sleepless nights as we tried to give him some assurance that he was safe and we would not let anything happen to him.

One night, Mark was so tormented that he was writhing on the floor in pain for hours, to the point that his ankles got carpet burns and started to bleed.

Often at night he would look out the window and say, "Don't you see them out there? They're in the trees. They are everywhere." When I asked Mark what he was seeing, he explained, "Slinky shapes lurking in the trees." Another night I had the television on and Mark said, "Shut it off, they're coming out of the TV at me." He also believed he was being sent messages through the radio.

I was terrified another time when I woke up not able to breathe. Mark was standing over me pressing extremely hard on my stomach, and Dave helped me push Mark away. Mark thought he was being perfectly clear with us as he explained that he was inside of me and he was trying to push himself out. After that incident, there were many nights we slept with our bedroom door locked. We had no idea what to make of Mark's behavior.

Dave and I were becoming extremely weary as we were not getting any consistent sleep. We were distraught and didn't know who to go to for help. We just didn't know what to do. It's pretty easy I suppose for someone to look at our situation and say, "Why didn't they just call someone for help?" But when you are up every night and trying to keep up with full-time jobs as well as following your youngest son's life and school events, after a while you just can't think straight.

Mark was dealing with an illness in his brain. As parents we were trying to come to terms with this illness and Mark did not want us telling anyone about it. We still did not know if Mark was going to his counseling appointments or if anyone had given him a diagnosis. Honestly, I was even afraid to try and ask Mark about the details of his health because I didn't want him to go into a full-blown psychotic episode again.

I just kept praying and, honestly, wondered if God was listening. I felt so alone. I just wanted someone I could talk to that understood what we were dealing with. I wished we had known about educational programs from groups like NAMI (National Alliance on Mental Illness) that are designed to help both an individual with mental illness and their family members understand the illness and the behaviors from such an illness.

Even though Mark did not want us discussing his condition with anyone else, Dave and I finally agreed we needed to enlist help from our church. Dave talked to his fellow deacons and shared about Mark's committal, the frustration in getting a diagnosis, the medical bills that were piling up, and the overall hopeless and helpless feelings we were experiencing. The deacons prayed with Dave and even helped pay for some of the hospital bills out of the special Deacon's Fund. Sharing this burden helped Dave and I feel that we were not quite so alone. Since Coach Ed Thomas was a deacon with Dave, and also our Sunday school leader, we began to update Ed each week after Sunday school class on how Mark was doing. Mark even started attending church with us, intermittently, and we could see he was trying hard to act in a way that we defined as "normal."

Mark continued to be plagued and tormented by the demons within and I finally contacted a man from our church who had offered to help us get in contact with a counselor at another church. Dave and I met with this counselor and explained to him what had been going on at home with Mark. We told him we just didn't know who to go to for help, who we could talk to that might understand Mark's behavior and what we, his parents, were going through. This counselor helped us set up an appointment with a local psychologist.

One night soon after, Mark called and said he had been arrested because he had gotten in a fight. He explained to us that he was trying to help a friend entangled in a fight. Mark's heart to help has always been bigger than his common sense. It made perfect sense, to Mark, to come to his friend's defense. We told Mark to call us when he was released from jail. Honestly, we didn't know what to believe anymore. I didn't want to have that attitude with Mark but just how many times could we go through these situations? Frankly, we knew Mark was probably safer in jail. It was a relief for me not to wonder where Mark was and if he was having psychotic episodes.

Dave and I were nervous and yet hopeful the day we met with the psychologist. Despite the interruptions as the doctor kept answering phone calls, we spent about half an hour explaining everything we had been going through with Mark and describing Mark's behavior in detail to him. We asked the psychologist what we should do when Mark was going through these episodes. We asked if there was a psychologist or psychiatrist he could recommend for Mark to see and if there was anyone that Dave and I could start seeing to help us through this turmoil. Even though Mark did not have medical insurance, Dave and I were willing to take on loans in order to get our son connected with someone who could actually help. We just didn't know who that someone should be!

After about an hour with this psychologist, his words to us were, "It sounds to me like you should get Mark signed up for disability, kick him out of the house, and he will eventually hook up with others like him." I was shocked by this suggestion! This was supposed to be the solution to the "help" we were so desperately seeking? In shock and silence Dave and I left that office and walked to the car. I told Dave, "I will never quit trying to get Mark the help he desperately needs and I am *not* going to kick him out of our home." Looking back now, I realize there comes a time when it is not feasible to have your loved one who is struggling with a brain illness live with you. But to receive that advice, that day, in that manner, was like a kick in the face to us. There has got to be a better way for a professional to communicate with his clients.

That same afternoon I contacted our local county's Central Point Coordinator (CPC) and left a message that I would like to set up a meeting with him to discuss Mark's committal, the follow-up counseling, and the medication he was supposed to be taking. One of the CPC's responsibilities is to assist residents in the county with mental illness to find services that will help them.

The CPC emailed me back and said he could meet the following week. However, due to the events that soon followed, this meeting never took place. Even though I was wrought with exhaustion and confusion, I should have followed through and sought help face-to-face with the CPC.

Mark's Erratic Behavior Escalates

Dave and I hadn't been home from the appointment with the psychologist very long when I received a phone call from Mark. "Mom, I'm out of jail. Can you pick me up?" I was apprehensive as I drove to Waterloo to pick up Mark. After the discouraging meeting with the psychologist I didn't know what to think. My mind was spinning in circles wondering how we could help our son. When I picked up Mark, he told me he was starving so I drove through McDonalds and picked up a burger and fries for him. As I proceeded to drive home, he began to explain to me the details of situation that had taken place with the friend he was trying to defend. In the middle of a sentence Mark abruptly stopped talking, almost as if he forgot where he was. As he turned toward me I could immediately tell by the glare on his face and his eyes boring into me that a psychotic episode was about to strike. Mark started a verbal attack against me. He yelled, "You c——, you whore, who do you think you are!" Fear filled me as I grabbed my cell phone and attempted to call Dave. Mark grabbed the phone out of my hand and broke it. He proceeded to hit me in the face and knocked my glasses off as I was driving down the road. I somehow pulled the car over and yelled at Mark, "Get out of this car right now!" I can't believe he listened to me. As I drove off he was swearing at me, calling me names, and kicking the car.

My whole body was shaking in shock and fear and disbelief. A few miles down the highway, I pulled the car over to the side of the road, grabbed the pieces of my cell phone, and somehow held them together long enough to get a phone call to my husband. I explained what had just happened. "Dave, call the sheriff's department and tell them about Mark. I don't want anyone stopping to pick up Mark while he is in this erratic state of mind." I drove home where Dave was waiting to comfort me. The sheriff called to let us know they couldn't find Mark anywhere.

Mark showed up at the house about an hour later. He remembered the episode saying, "Mom, I'm so sorry. I didn't mean to hurt you. I don't know what came over me. I'm so tired. Can I just go to bed?" Mark looked dejected and sad. I know he didn't mean to hurt me or do anything to me. I think he was as confused by his behavior as I was. He went to bed and actually slept. I, on the other hand, slept with one eye and ear open all night. I was afraid of Mark—afraid of my own son.

Two days later, on my birthday, Mark was overtaken with yet another full-blown psychotic episode. He started yelling, "You whore! Dave isn't even my father. That's what's wrong with me. It's your fault."

Dave got mad at the accusations Mark was hurling toward me. Mark turned on him and said, "Let's go to the hospital right now. I want a paternity test. Prove to me that you're my father." Dave told Mark that he would go to the hospital but that he just needed to calm down and quit treating his mom this way. As Mark continued the tirade, Dave was angry at what Mark was saying about me and the two of them physically wrestled. Dave finally hugged and held Mark tightly until he could feel his body give in. Mark again said, "I'm better off dead!" He stormed out of the house and didn't come back that night. We had heard Mark make this type of threat in the past, but on this night would he actually follow through with it? In utter despair, we prayed.

The next morning I called Mark's attorney who handled the original committal hearing to report to her the episodes from the past couple months. Since this attorney represented Mark and could not act on my behalf, she recommended I call the hospital of committal and report to them what was happening. I proceeded to do so and as I explained to them

Mark's most recent episodes, I believe I was really looking for answers to our questions.

- "Is Mark supposed to be taking medication?"
- "Is Mark supposed to be seeing a counselor?"
- "Is he showing up for his appointments?"
- "Has Mark received a diagnosis yet?"
- "Is anyone reporting to the courts that Mark is, or is not, complying with the court ordered treatment?"
- "Who is making sure my son is getting the help he needs?"
- "How are we supposed to help our son and keep ourselves and Mark safe?"

It wasn't long before the county sheriff's department called me and asked if I knew where Mark was. They told me that they had an order from the hospital to bring Mark back in.

It was midmorning when I saw Mark's car making its way up the driveway. I was afraid and didn't want Mark to see me, so I went to my bedroom and locked the door until I heard him stomp downstairs. I quickly got in my car and drove to a parking lot near our house and called Dave, who in turn, called the sheriff's department. Once again, tears streamed down my face as I watched my son being taken away in the sheriff's car. All I could think about was, *Lord, where are you? Why can't you help our son? I beg you, Lord, help us! Help Mark!*

After I got back home, I had mixed emotions as I called the county CPC to discuss Mark's behavior, the first committal, and now this order to bring Mark back into the hospital. The CPC told me he "didn't remember the paper work crossing his desk" but that he would call the hospital and meet with Mark. The CPC called me later that night and asked me a lot of questions about Mark, from the time he was conceived to current day. He wanted to know all about Mark's childhood and history. After this conversation, despite being frustrated at our son's "paper work" issue, I thought to myself that, finally, something is happening here. Someone is listening.

The Second Time Around

This time we did not visit Mark at the hospital. We decided to let the doctors work with Mark and just stay out of the process. What a dilemma. My family's annual Christmas gathering was going up, which we always held over Thanksgiving weekend. Despite the crushing despair that faced us, Dave and I knew it was important for at least me to go with our other two sons, Brad and Scott, to the family Christmas. Dave stayed home just in case Mark needed us to come to the hospital. I didn't go into details with my family about Mark's episodes, only that he was in the hospital as we were desperately seeking answers for our son's illness. What a lonely weekend that had to be for Dave. And, even though

I was surrounded by loving family, I felt incredibly alone and sad as well.

Mark was released from the hospital five days later, and Dave and I went to the courthouse for the hearing. Once again it's interesting that we were not allowed to be in the hearing, but it was okay for the assistant county attorney to ask us if we would be willing to take Mark home to stay with us. We agreed Mark could come back home but we wanted to know what the details of Mark's treatment plan was going to be and where he was supposed to go for help. Mark was angry at the ultimatum the attorney presented to him. He either could come home with us or he could be sent to another facility.

We really needed someone with expertise who could listen to what we were living with and who could tell us the best course of action to take with Mark. Mark also needed someone to advocate for him and protect his interests. What we did not know at the time was that the court should have provided Mark with a Mental Health Advocate. He was not.

Mark did come home with us but there are times that I wonder if our decision was the right one.

I called the county CPC when we arrived home and asked him what was being done for Mark and who he was supposed to be seeing. Do we assume Mark will be taking medication? Who is responsible for paying for that medicine? Who is responsible for making sure he would go to his appointments and take his meds? So many questions and no concrete answers. The CPC said he would meet with Mark and help him get all of these items set up. I then asked the CPC, "Do you think it would be a good move for Mark if we provided a place for him to stay that is out of our house? Dave and I are thinking that maybe Mark needs some space away from us and that some independence would be good for him." I went on to explain that I didn't know if my presence was causing some of Mark's behavior but I did know that Mark living with us wasn't working for him, or for us, and that we were at our wit's end. The CPC said he didn't see that Mark staying somewhere else for a while would hurt Mark in any way. He seemed to understand our frustration at this point.

It was going on six months since Mark had moved back home from South Dakota. Our lives felt so very dark. We kept encountering these storms, and I really couldn't see the light. I felt like Mark, Dave, and I were in the middle of a cyclone that kept throwing us around and around but we were not making any progress. I just wanted this spinning to stop.

7

SO CLOSE, YET SO FAR

After Mark was home for a few days, Dave and I sat down with Mark and explained to him that we were trying to listen and understand what he was going through.

"Mark, Dad and I sense that you need your independence. Would you be interested in staying at a hotel that allows extended stays?" Mark was very interested in that arrangement. I went on to say, "Mark, we are willing to help pay for this, but we do have some expectations of you. You need to follow through with everything your counselor asks you to do including taking prescribed medications. You also need to start looking for a part-time job." Mark appeared to be relieved to try something different. We took him to a hotel that allowed long-term stays and paid for a month in advance.

Although this seemed like the right thing to do at the time, it was an anguishing decision. I was worried that Mark would get lost in his illness and who would take care of him then? On the other hand, I anticipated both Dave and I would finally get caught up on some much-needed rest. Who was I kidding? So many hours in the middle of the night were spent in prayer for Mark's healing and protection. I just wanted to see Mark happy and without pain.

Meanwhile, Dave and I continued to try and keep up with our jobs and to give our other two sons some attention, which they greatly deserved. We had been trying to shield Scott and Brad from these episodes the best we could but it was starting to place a strain on them too. The travel requirements of my job continued and it was becoming quite strenuous to have this stress going on at home and still trying to keep it all together. Perhaps having Mark live elsewhere would give us a chance to regroup and get our lives together.

We continued to apprise Coach Thomas each week after Sunday school on how things were going with Mark. He expressed his concern to us and encouraged us to keep the faith. Ed continued to uplift us in prayer.

Christmas Day – Trying to Shake Off the Sadness

This time that Mark lived away from us at the extended hotel turned out to be a very dark period in Mark's life. The times Dave, Scott, and I tried to visit Mark, go out to eat with him, or take him to a movie, turned out to be hit or miss whether he would be in one of his "episodes." I didn't know if he was making it to his appointments. I kept trying to encourage him and, above all, pray that things would get better.

Christmas day arrived that year and turned out to be very sad for me. Mark missed the family meal entirely. We waited until he showed up midafternoon to open gifts. Tension filled the air when he was in the house. When Mark opened up our gift to him he glared at me, tossed the gift on the counter, and stormed out of the house. Our gift was a practical one: six months paid auto insurance. Finances were tight and debt was piling up as we were paying for some of Mark's hospital bills, housing, and student loan payments. Mark didn't have health insurance.

Christmas in our family is about celebrating Jesus' birth. We know the gift of salvation each one of us has been given when Jesus died on the cross for us to take away our sins. It's about spending time together as a family.

One day shortly after Christmas, I saw Mark arrive at our farm. It's sad to admit that I had taken to hiding in my bedroom until I could ascertain what kind of state Mark was in. I was chilled when he walked through the kitchen door and I heard him say, "I can smell her, where is she?" I ventured out to the kitchen and asked Mark what he was talking about. Instead of answering my question directly, he said that whenever he comes in the house he can *feel and smell* the evil, especially in the stairwell. Was this actually my son, Mark, expressing these random, dark thoughts? Where in Mark's brain were these bizarre ideas coming from?

Spring Brings Hope . . . or Not

After about eight weeks it was getting too expensive for us to continue paying for Mark to stay at a hotel so we had no choice but to bring him home. The next couple months brought spring weather and it seemed to bring a new life to Mark as well. Although we observed Mark still struggling with the voices and delusions, the episodes didn't seem as extreme and Mark seemed more willing to talk about how he was feeling. He started going to church again and also began an exercise routine including walking, jogging, and lifting weights. It appeared Mark was getting a new lease on life and that he might be going to some counseling appointments.

Perhaps spring was just what we all needed. I finally felt our prayers were being answered. I, again, kept thinking Mark would "snap out of it" and simply be "our" Mark again . . . I often wish that it had been explained to us that someone with an illness like Mark's would never just "snap out of it." This would be an illness Mark, and everyone who loved him, would live with the rest of his life. We didn't even know a diagnosis at this time, so we were in the dark about all of it.

On Easter Sunday, I invited my parents to come for lunch. We had the full holiday meal fixings: ham, mashed potatoes, corn, and dinner rolls. Everyone took a little snooze after eating such a big meal. Midafternoon my folks, Dave, Mark, and I were sitting around the dining room table having cake and ice cream and visiting. With no warning Mark turned his head, looked down the hallway, turned back again, and was overcome with a full-blown psychotic episode. Mark's facial features looked different, his voice sounded different, his body language was aggressive and vulgar. He started yelling at us, "Quit looking at me that way! What's wrong with you people?" As Mark continued into a full-scale episode, I tried to rush my parents out of the house to safety. My dad didn't want to leave me and he kept saying that I had to get away as well.

Dave got Mark out of the house at the same time my twin sister and her two daughters happened to arrive. What a mess! Although our families knew we were having problems with Mark, we had not even attempted to explain the degree of severity his illness had escalated to. We just kept hoping that Mark was going to finally come out of it and, for a few weeks, it actually appeared he had been getting better.

Needless to say, we proceeded to get my family off the farm and I followed shortly thereafter as Dave was concerned for my safety. He stayed with Mark to try and calm him down. I went to a friend in town who was a nurse. She was somewhat aware of what we had been going through with Mark. After explaining what had taken place, my friend encouraged me to call the emergency number for the agency where Mark was seeing a counselor. When the on-call counselor called me back, I explained that Mark was having a severe episode and asked him what we should do. The counselor's response to me was, "What do you want me to do? I've never seen Mark. He's not my patient." In desperation

I asked the counselor if they would just try and talk to Mark on the phone and they told me to call the sheriff or take him to the emergency room. My frustration at the lack of assistance was mounting. However, why should I expect that a counselor could reach Mark's mind through a phone call? I just wanted to feel like someone empathized and understood what we were going through.

We had tried the hospital committal route two times and as far as we could tell we were no closer to a diagnosis for Mark than we were seven months ago. We decided to call the sheriff and one of the deputies came out. After some time the deputy managed to calm Mark down. The deputy did talk to Dave and me and stated that it appeared that whenever I was present it seemed to exacerbate Mark. The deputy thought it would be best for me to leave the house whenever we could see Mark was going to have an episode. This was crushing for me to hear. Do you have any idea what it feels like for a mother to have to leave her home . . . to leave her husband and sons? All of our lives were spinning out of control and we didn't know where to turn for help.

What Is It Going to Take?

The next day I called the agency where Mark's court order had referred him for treatment and asked to speak with his counselor. I was told the counselor was not in. I explained the episode of the day before to the person on the phone and they said they would report the details of this incident to Mark's counselor. A few days later, I still had not heard back from the counselor, so I tried to reach her again. I was told the counselor was out of the office but that a message would be given to her.

A few days later, I was out of town working and Dave called me and said that Mark had asked him to take him to the hospital. He repeated what Mark had said to him, "Dad, I have so much pain and I think I'm dying." I quickly wrapped up my work at the client site and began the long drive home. My mind flipped back and forth between worry for Mark and praying for his healing. I arrived home only to find that the hospital ran some tests and sent Mark home. We didn't know the results of these tests. HIPPA was the reason we kept hearing we couldn't get information about our son's health conditions.

The next day, I called Mark's counselor again and was actually able to speak with her. She was extremely reluctant to talk with me but I told her, "You don't have to say a word about what has been taking place between you and Mark, but you are going to listen to what our family and our son have been going through." After explaining everything that had been happening she stated she wasn't aware of the Easter Sunday incident or of any other episodes Mark was having. I basically told her, "Why would you be? He is probably only showing up for appointments when he is in a lucid state, not when he is in a full-blown episode!" I went on to say that it had been way too long since Mark had had contact with her. She then explained that she can't make an appointment for Mark but told me that Mark could call in to schedule an appointment to see her. I wondered how much luck I was going to have convincing my son, who didn't think anything was wrong with him, to call and make this appointment.

A couple weeks later Mark had another horrible episode. He said he was going to call 911 to report that we, his parents, were abusing him. He was yelling at us, using many of the same verbal attacks he had yelled at us during previous episodes. These attacks were like a broken record that kept repeating itself over and over again. What I didn't realize is that Mark really did call 911. Shortly after he hung up the phone I received a call on my cell phone from the dispatcher and she told me, "Joan, we heard the whole dialogue, help is on the way!"

The sheriff's department sent three deputies to our aid that night. I called the county CPC and the deputy spoke with him and explained the situation. The CPC said we could commit Mark again or take him to the emergency room. I asked the CPC that night, "What is it going to take to get our son the help he so desperately needs?" What haunts me was the silence on the telephone line as, sadly, the CPC had no answer for me.

The deputies stayed with Mark until they could calm him down and again suggested it would be wise for me to leave the house when Mark was around. From that day forward, if Mark came around I packed a bag and left. It's a good thing

I have a lot of family all over the state I could call on at a moment's notice to go and stay with. I spent many hours driving during this time in my life and on many of these trips I would sob so deeply that I would have to pull the car off the road until I could regain composure to drive safely. I was incredibly sad, confused, and frustrated at trying to find help for my son. I just felt like doors were being slammed in my face and I was losing hope of ever finding the answers I so desperately needed.

Ups and Downs

A couple days later, the county CPC called me and said he had changed the court order for Mark to receive treatment at a different agency. Within a couple days, two people from the new agency contacted me and asked for Mark's cell phone number so they could arrange an appointment with him. Within a few weeks, the new agency had helped Mark move to an apartment in Waterloo and he began working with new counselors at this agency. In the meantime, Mark had applied for job as a baker at a new restaurant in Cedar Falls. He was so happy when he got this job. He was finally feeling like he had some self-worth. In addition, he contracted to mow the lawn at our local township cemetery. We were so proud of Mark and he seemed happy to be working again. I was excited and relieved at the progress Mark was making. Mark just wanted someone to believe him, listen to him, and he really did want help. The real Mark underneath all of this suffering did not want to be living with these inexplicable episodes. I felt like the sun was beginning to shine again.

An illness in the brain is deceitful. Talk about highs and lows. Not just for the individual with the illness, but for their loved ones as well. During these months there were actually some highs mixed in with the lows. Mark began helping Dave with projects on the farm. We would begin to get our hopes up only to have them crash to the ground again during the next episode. I recall one day just getting in the car and driving just to escape the house during one of Mark's episodes. I was so weary and tired. I screamed and cried out to God to heal Mark. Dave and I continued to rely on our faith in God because that is the only thing that continued to sustain us and give us hope. Although we could see Mark was making progress with this new agency, he was still suffering.

Early in June, I received a phone call from yet another hospital in our area stating Mark had come in to their emergency room. They wanted to know our address so they could send the bill. No, we could not find out why Mark visited the emergency room; they just wanted us to provide the address to them. I found it interesting that the hospital could talk to us about where to send a bill but we weren't allowed to know what was wrong with our son or why he had gone into the emergency room.

Just a couple days later our neighbor called me and said Mark had stopped by their place looking for her husband,

Glen (not his real name). Mark told our neighbor's wife
he was really hurting and needed to talk to someone. She
told Mark that Glen was at work but that there were some
counselors down at church camp getting things ready for
camp. This neighbor's farm was where Mark had attended
church camp many years earlier. Mark went to the camp area
and spoke with a couple of the counselors. Our pastor told
us later that he had been called to come and talk to Mark. By
the time he arrived it appeared the counselors were praying
with Mark and he didn't want to interfere. I can relate to
how the pastor felt that day as sometimes Dave and I didn't
even know how to respond to Mark's episodes. We must
remember that much of the brain continues to be a mystery
to which only God holds the key. Who are we to think we can
understand something so intricate and complex?

Things in Mark's life were starting to escalate again. Just
a couple days later, Dave called me and said it had been
a rough evening. He shared that when he got home from
work Mark asked Dave if he would help him load up the
lawn mower so he could mow the township cemetery. Dave
went to fuel up the mower. He was driving up to the shed
and looked up just in time to see Mark running toward
him. Mark threw himself at Dave, knocking him off the
mower. It's a good thing Dave is a strong man and was able
to overtake Mark and stop the attack. Dave held him tight
and talked calmly to him until he could feel Mark give in.
Mark stood up and headed up the driveway to his car. Dave

started walking up the driveway and glanced up just as Mark was throwing a rock at him. Mark then got in his car and sped out of the yard.

Urgently I told Dave, "Call the agency that is working with Mark and report the details of this incident. They need to know what's going on." He proceeded to do so and the agency told Dave they would report the issue to Mark's counselor. The agency went on to say, "We have been working with Mark and he has been communicating to us about his out-of-body experiences, the delusions, and the voices he has been hearing. Our team has determined that Mark is probably dealing with paranoid schizophrenia. We are in the process of arranging an appointment for Mark with a psychiatrist so they can confirm this diagnosis and get Mark started on medication."

The next week or so was amazingly quiet. One night Mark stopped by and we all walked down to the gazebo that we loved to relax in, looking out over our pond. A conversation started and Mark apologized to his dad about the lawn mowing incident. Mark said, "Dad, it wasn't me attacking you. I was up in the air watching my body doing these things and I had no control over it." Dave and I encouraged Mark to keep communicating with his counselors and with us. We reassured him that we loved him and we were there for him.

High-Speed Chase

About a week later, around 8:30 p.m., Mark stopped by
the house and drank an ice tea with Dave and me. It was a
beautiful summer evening, and he told us he was just out for
a drive and wanted to stop by and say hello. We visited for a
few minutes and Mark told us he had had a great day before
he said good-bye and drove off.

One hour later, our county sheriff called me and said,
"Joan, I just wanted to let you know that Mark is okay."

I replied, "I know he is okay, he was just here an hour ago
and had an ice tea with us."

Incredulous, the sheriff went on to explain that Mark
had driven to a house about twenty miles away from us.
He confronted the owner of the house (the father of one of
Mark's former classmates) and started hitting their front
door with a baseball bat. The homeowner called 911 and
Mark took off in his car. A high-speed chase ensued west
on gravel roads, then through the town of Parkersburg,
and ended just north of our house where Mark hit a deer
on the highway. The sheriff told us it was a good thing he
had arrived when he did so he could get everyone else to
back down because the law enforcement on the scene had
their guns drawn. Apparently, after the accident happened,
Mark barreled out of the car in a full-blown psychotic rage.
The sheriff knew of Mark's mental health history and tried
to get Mark transported to the hospital of Mark's original
committal, but there were no beds available. The sheriff

did manage to get Mark committed to a different hospital's mental health unit.

The sheriff followed up with us Sunday morning to let us know Mark was in the hospital and that it would probably be five to seven days before he would be released. I felt such relief knowing Mark was safe. As a parent, it is so frightening to know that at any moment your son could have an episode and be out of control like that. Dave and I didn't want anyone, including our son, to be hurt and I thanked God for the miracle that Mark hadn't hit anyone with his car during the chase.

Dave and I entered church that morning with very heavy hearts. We were sure many people had heard about the high-speed chase. Although we did not feel like facing people, we knew we needed God and fellowship with other believers.

What I did not know was that Mark's medical records from the first hospital of committal did not follow him to this hospital. I wonder to this day whose responsibility it is for informing a different medical facility about Mark's prior medical history of mental illness. Mark was certainly in no state of mind to share that information. Should the psychiatrist at this hospital have looked into Mark's medical history more thoroughly? I realize there are too many unanswered questions.

On Monday morning I called and spoke with the individual who had been working with Mark from the support services agency and explained the weekend events.

That night the counselor called me back and said that Mark had signed a release form so that he could discuss treatment details with us. This was the first time in this whole process of dealing with Mark's illness that we were made aware that an information release form was an option. The counselor told me the hospital had put Mark on two medications. I said, "Wait a minute. Will these medications conflict with the ones the psychiatrist has prescribed for Mark?"

The counselor quietly responded, "Joan, Mark hasn't seen a psychiatrist yet. That appointment is scheduled for about a month from now. We can't get him in before then." I couldn't hold back my disbelief that despite all of the events that had taken place, which we felt were extremely dangerous to Mark, to us, and to others, that they could not get Mark in to see a psychiatrist immediately.

I went on to discuss the lawn-mowing incident with the counselor and he stated that Mark had mentioned he had an argument with his dad but that he was unaware of the lawn mowing incident. Apparently, the message I left with the agency also got lost in the shuffle. I was getting pretty used to the lack of communication.

I asked the counselor if we should try and visit Mark or if we should just stay away for a while. The counselor said, "I tell you what, let me just work with Mark for a while. I'll let you know when Mark is doing better and you can visit him." Sad to say, again I felt a sense of relief. I wasn't sure how much more I could take of this roller coaster.

In the meantime, Jan Thomas, who worked at City Hall, called me and told me someone had stopped by and turned in Mark's driver's license. He had found it on a walk that morning. Jan is Coach Thomas's wife and we went to church together. I actually opened up a bit and spent a little time sharing our frustration at trying to get Mark the help he needed with his mental illness. I told her I was thankful that Mark would be at the hospital for a while and that just maybe we could get him some much-needed help.

I'll Call . . . Again and Again

Less than three days after Mark had been admitted to the hospital, I received a phone call from Mark. "Mom, I'm out of the hospital and I'm locked out of my apartment. Can I stay with you and dad tonight?"

I was so confused. What was I to do? Mark's counselor had told us to stay away from Mark, yet here was our son, released from the hospital, out on the streets in Waterloo, and locked out of his apartment. I told Mark to stay put and that we would find someone to pick him up.

I tried to call the agency to speak with Mark's counselor and received an answering service. I was told to call back after 8:15 a.m. the next morning. Dave and I started the forty-five minute drive to Waterloo. I again called the agency, "We have a situation here and I need to speak with Mark Becker's counselor. Mark has been released from the hospital and his counselor has asked us not to see Mark until we get the go-ahead from him. We really need to talk to him!" The answering service repeated that I could call back the next morning after 8:15 a.m.

Dave and I had so many questions. The sheriff had told us Mark would be in the hospital five to seven days. Why was Mark released from the hospital so soon? Who picked Mark up from the hospital? We figured since Mark had been in the high-speed chase that the hospital would be releasing Mark to the authorities. Didn't they submit paper work to the hospital? Again, there were so many unanswered questions.

Dave and I picked up Mark. We stopped by Mark's workplace so he could get his work schedule and pick up his paycheck. On the drive home Mark explained to us his recollection of the high-speed chase. He said, "I was up in the air watching the cars driving on the road below. I was in a coffin that was closed but someone kept opening it up and helping me get out of the coffin." Mark then told us he felt like God was telling him he still had work to do. I got goose bumps from the fear that gripped me. Where was Mark's mind taking him?

Dave and I had no idea what to think of this. On the drive home we prayed with Mark. After a quick stop at the convenience store in Parkersburg, we finally walked in the house close to midnight and all of us went to bed to try and get some sleep. However, sleep did not come to Dave and I. We were up most of the night trying to decide what we should do the next day. I told Dave I was not comfortable being alone at the house with Mark. After much discussion, we decided I would work at my office in Ames and Dave would go to work to get his mechanics set up for the day. He would then pick up Mark's apartment keys from the sheriff's department and take Mark to Waterloo. After that, Dave and I spent time praying for Mark and for the whole situation. We were desperate for answers. We just needed help. Mark needed help. Where could we turn?

8

THE CATACLYSM

June 24, 2009. I was already up getting ready for work when Mark knocked on our bedroom door at five asking how many scoops of coffee it took to make a pot of coffee. Although weary from lack of sleep I knew I wanted to be out of the house before Dave left for work. Scott had already left to finish his weight lifting for the day before he went to work.

I heard Dave and Mark discussing the schedule for the day. I was encouraged when I heard Mark ask if there was anyone in town who still needed help with tornado cleanup. Dave said, "Mark, you can help in town another day, but you can't drive anywhere today. How about you spend some time picking up sticks around here? We got quite a storm the other night and the yard needs to be picked up before we can mow." Dave went on to explain that he would go to work, get his mechanics going for the day, stop by the sheriff's office to get Mark's apartment keys, and then come home to drive Mark back to Waterloo.

I called Dave when I got on the road and reminded him to pull the keys from the old Chevy Lumina we had sitting around as a spare car. Dave did pull the keys and took them to work. We both knew it was critical that Mark did not get behind the wheel and drive after the high-speed chase incident.

I'm not quite sure I can even remember the hour and a half drive to Ames that early morning as my thoughts were so intent on Mark—the frustration of finding adequate help for him, the anger at the lack of communication . . . all of it! I kept wracking my brain trying to figure out where we could go to get someone to understand how hopeless we felt with the situation with Mark.

I began my morning at work talking on the phone with a client when all of a sudden my cell phone started going crazy with calls and text messages coming in. *That's weird. I wonder what's going on.* I quickly finished up my call with the client and immediately another worker in my office came running up to my desk saying, "Joan, did you hear? Coach Thomas has been shot!" She didn't have any other details.

My brain started swirling as I worried about Ed. The episode from nine months earlier started playing out in my head when Mark was on the tirade thinking that Ed, Dave, and I were all in a conspiracy trying to poison the minds of the children in our community. Surely Mark's mind didn't snap to this extent! As I was trying to grasp what I had just been told, I called Dave to ask if he had heard about Coach

Thomas. Dave was quiet and then said, "Joan, do you think you can get your brother to drive you home? It appears Mark is involved with the shooting. You need to come to the sheriff's office so they can ask you some questions."

I dropped the phone and my body began to tremble and shake uncontrollably. I remember my head falling to my desk. I started moaning and saying, "No, it can't be possible. We have tried so hard to get Mark help . . . this can't be happening."

My manager came to my side and picked up my phone, rubbing my shoulders trying to find out what had happened. My phone rang and it was Mark's counselor. He said, "Joan, how ya doing?" I answered flatly, "How do you think I'm doing? I tried to call you last night and they wouldn't let me talk to you." He responded, "Yeah, we're looking into that right now." He said he would try to find out what Ed's condition was and get back to me.

My manager moved me to a private office where I started to sob uncontrollably. The prior long horrendous nine months flashed before my eyes. It was almost as if every episode, every desperate plea for help, the yelling, the pain . . . all of it was racing around in my mind. My head was throbbing with pain but the rest of my body was numb.

Another phone call jarred me, "Joan, this is Pamela. Does Scott know about Coach Thomas?" I said that I hadn't called him yet. I felt horrible that I hadn't even thought to call him yet. Pamela was a close friend and like a second mom to Scott. I told her, "I think Scott is still at the lumberyard working." After she hung up, she immediately drove to the lumberyard to be at Scott's side as she shared with him the devastating news.

My brother, Mike, arrived at my office and helped me to the car. I'll never forget that trip as long as I live. One of my brother's pastors called and prayed with me, and my brother prayed with me. Selfishly, I was praying, "God, if we can't have Ed back with his whole mind and body just the way he was before, can you spare his family and Ed the grief of any more pain?" I just kept praying over and over for Ed, Jan, Ed's boys and their families and, yes, I was praying for my son Mark.

About half way home I received another phone call from Mark's counselor, "Joan, Ed Thomas passed away." I alternated the remainder of that drive between repeating to my brother over and over, "We have tried so hard to get Mark help. Why did it come to this?" and praying fervently for the Thomas family.

Here is my husband Dave's recollection from that tragic day:

We went to bed about midnight. Sleep didn't come quickly. I was confused about why Mark had been released after the high-speed chase and all (No charges?). It seemed like I had just

dozed off for a second before I was awakened
by Mark asking me if it took two or three scoops
of coffee to make a full pot. He wanted to have
coffee with me before I went to work. I told
him three scoops. I sat on the edge of the bed
thinking, yes, I needed coffee if I was going to
function at all . . . clueless about what this day
had in store for me.

Mark's conversation with me centered around
there being a balance in life (good things, bad
things). I remember he used an analogy about
a teeter-totter; ups and downs to find a balance.
He said the tornado was a bad thing but all the
good was coming out of the stories of people
helping others. Mark was very philosophical that
morning, and I thought to myself that this was
the result of some of his counseling. He was
using psychological terms to explain things, not
exactly his normal vocabulary. I chalked it up
once again to the fact that he had been talking
mostly to counselors lately at the hospital.

The plans were laid out. I was going to talk
to Sheriff Johnson about the car keys, mainly
the apartment key that was on the key ring in
the impounded vehicle's ignition. That being
said, deep down I was sure Sheriff Johnson was
going to want to arrest Mark for the high-speed

chase. Mark was adamant that he wanted to help someone in need and asked if I knew of any projects going on. I more or less humored him and told him of a couple that I had heard of still needing help, but that for a couple hours this morning I told him he could pick up some branches on the yard. I said that would be a big help to me and he agreed.

So I headed off to work and said I would be back as soon as I got my guys started. I was sick with the fact that we were once again up against a wall. There was going to be jail time, fines, and no driver's license for a long time. Transportation to and from work and appointments were all going to be a hassle.

Joan and I had exhausted our savings and bank accounts with the medical expenses of the committals, emergency room visits, and housing costs we had been trying to assume. The thought I couldn't quite let go of was the conversation I had had on the church steps last Sunday with one of the officials that had been on the scene after Mark had hit the deer which ended the high-speed chase. He said Mark had once again tested clean of any drugs. This official went on to say that since he grew up with mental illness in his family (his mother) he was going to go to bat for us and help us get Mark some help. Is this what was going on since there were no charges filed?

This was what was always hard. When Mark was himself he was caring, loving, concerned about others, and sympathetic about people's feelings. He was just a great person. That he could change in a heartbeat and scare you about how he thought things should be dealt with was not the Mark . . . the son I knew and loved. If you haven't ever experienced one of these episodes you wouldn't understand. We had even secretly tape-recorded some of the dialogue once so we could try to explain what we were experiencing.

So when I got to work I made the phone call to the sheriff's office and was told as soon as the sheriff got in he would give me a call. The morning whiled away as usual. Did the parts show up for the mower tractor, is the tandem done, do we need to order culverts? Finally the phone rang (deep sigh). "Hello," my neighbor said, "Yeah neighbor, you might want to run home and see what's going on. I saw a couple of squad cars fly up your driveway. Word in town is somebody shot Coach Thomas."

As I drove home I happened to meet one of
the squad cards. I looked over and saw Mark in
the backseat of the squad car. My first thought
was, did some lowlife shoot Coach and come to
our house? Along the way, some of Mark's old
acquaintances were nonathletes and thought
AP football and Coach Thomas were overrated.
Oh buddy, I hope you didn't have anything
to do with it or know anything about it. But
they are probably just bringing everyone in for
questioning. As I pulled up the driveway I could
see a squad car in the driveway. It was parked
behind the old Chevy Lumina we had had
parked for some time trying to decide whether
or not to fix it. It still ran, but barely. I don't even
remember if it had plates on anymore.

Beside the car on the ground by the driver's
door lay my dad's revolver. It was the one dad
had gotten when I was a young boy. As a boy, I
would target shoot on Sunday afternoons trying
to become a good shot with a handgun. Then
one day after we were married, Dad said, "Why
don't you take that gun home? You shot it the
most of anyone (of my four brothers)." I had been
so excited to have it because of the memories I
had of it. But now, confused and my mind going
a hundred miles an hour, things were lining up

wrong and the reality was soaking in. The officer was walking toward me as I opened the truck door. What the heck happened I thought? How could it possibly come to this? I don't remember the exact conversation but somehow the officer revealed to me that Mark was the shooter. My next recollections are just a series of still frame pictures going through my mind: the car, the gun, my house, my neighbor standing there, and the officer. The silence was then broken by the officer asking me to get in the squad car. He was supposed to bring me in also. The Division of Criminal Investigation (DCI) agent wanted to ask a few questions.

On the six-mile drive back to the sheriff's office I remember thinking, "This must be what it's like to be in denial while having a heart attack . . . warning signs missed, chest pains will go away!" I will feel better in a little bit. I didn't think it could ever come to this. Mark had mentioned Ed in one of the early episodes but never had an obsession with any one person. It was usually situations in history, like the Christian Crusades and Europe. It might be something with Hitler and Germany. It was always something about how people are pushing their agenda on others. I would usually sit and

listen to hear him out and he would eventually
give it up and slowly come to his senses, back
to the normal Mark. These episodes exhausted
both Mark and me. Where did I fail as his father?

The car stopped in front of the sheriff's office.
As I entered the office the gals all seemed very
busy. As a county employee myself, I knew
everyone on a first-name basis. No one looked up.
"Let's use this office," I was told. As I entered,
they informed me Scott was on his way also. I
called my wife and asked her if she could arrange
a way home from where she was working. I hung
up and prayed, "Be with me, Lord, and my family."
Numbness started setting in.

Scott showed up. We hugged and prayed
out loud together. "The DCI agent is ready to
interview you now. Come with us." The agent
was my in-law's neighbor, Chris. I had talked
with him on several occasions over the years.
The interview started. The questions were
routine. Yes, the revolver was locked up in a
cabinet. I had nothing to hide nor would I. Next
it was Scott. I told Scott it wasn't hard; just
tell them what you know. Sometime later Joan
walked in the room. We embraced, tears rolling
down our cheeks as we held each other tight.
Scott had returned from his interview and the

three of us sat with our hands joined, taking turns praying out loud. We all knew that our lives had taken a huge change and we didn't understand why. But we did know that we weren't on this journey of life alone. We had our Lord and Savior Jesus Christ by our sides to help us through. As I look back to that day, in many aspects the day that started with, "Hey, Dad, two scoops or three?" has not yet ended.

Family and friends surrounded us that day. A group of our friends from church parked themselves at the end of the driveway protecting our home from the media. Scott had left the weight room shortly before the shooting occurred and had heard something happened at the high school but didn't know the details until Pamela talked to him. She took Scott home with her and it wasn't long before our neighbor picked up Scott and drove him to the sheriff's office.

Here are recollections from that fateful day as written by my youngest son, Scott:

June 24, 2009, was a day full of unexpected happenings. First, two of my best friends visited me at work about something abnormal that happened at the school. One of those friends was in agony, unlike anything I had ever seen before. When I asked him what was really going on down at that bus barn, he said, "My mom is coming over to talk to you."

Next I walked outside of work seeking answers only to see a carload of my buddies saying, "Sorry Scott, are you all right?" which led to more questions. I said, "Yeah, I'm all right, what is going on?" and I thought to myself, "Something is up." Immediately, my friend's mom showed up and said with urgency, "Guys! He doesn't know. Let me talk to him first." She then sat me down and I was thinking, "This is not normal." Then she steadily told me, "Coach Thomas has been shot." I said something I didn't even anticipate. "It was Mark, wasn't it?"

I never thought Mark would hurt anybody because that just wasn't Mark, but I also never expected Mark would someday have paranoid schizophrenia. I soon figured Mark wasn't himself when he was having psychotic episodes. I never expected Mark in his right mind to do something like he did because, simply put, that wasn't Mark. At the same time I never knew what to expect when Mark wasn't in his right mind when he was in an episode of paranoid schizophrenia. June 24, 2009, was full of unexpected happenings, but fortunately, that is not where the story ends.

The Cataclysm

I never expected later on to get hundreds
of messages all basically saying, "We love
you, Scott, we are here for you," on the same
day of the shooting. From those closest to
Coach, to those who didn't know me but knew
what I was going through. I never expected
Aaron Thomas to say, "Reach out and pray
for the Becker family." I never expected Aaron
and Todd Thomas to say to me, "If you need
anything, we're here for you, we love you." That
is the most powerful action of God's grace
working through man toward me that I've ever
witnessed.

I never expected Coach's legacy (but mostly
God's legacy) to be so big that many people
around the world would be affected positively
from such a negative event. I never expected
high profile celebrities and athletes at the ESPY's
(Excellent in Sports Yearly Award presented by
the American cable television network ESPN) to
be brought to tears by a positive message (told
by Aaron) from a negative event. I never expected
to see my mom speak about mental illness all
over Iowa. I never expected I would be telling
my story to people I had just met and to classes
of middle school children. I never expected to be
able to teach about adversity and faith or relate

to those with connections to mental illness. I never expected my brother to get the help he needed, long after my parents' many attempts, even though it was later than I would have liked. When people ask me, "How did you do it?" I never expected I would answer, "Through God working in me," because I was so frustrated with God at first. I never expected so much good to come out of so much bad from the day of June 24, 2009. Would I want all this good to happen at the expense of so many people including my brother and coach? No, but ultimately it's not mine or anybody else's story to write.

When I arrived at the sheriff's department, I met up with Dave and Scott. The DCI agent shared what details he could of how Mark had gone into the weight room and shot Coach Thomas. I remember asking the agent, "How is Mark?" I did not ask if I could talk to Mark because I didn't even want to see the person that took the life of another person that day. I knew in my heart that it was not the Mark we knew and loved that could have even done that act, but the psychotic person that emerged during the deepest and darkest of delusional attacks.

We spent all afternoon at the sheriff's office, each of us being questioned. Isn't it strange that the very individuals who helped us the most during Mark's psychotic episodes were the same people having to live this nightmare with us now? I guess this would be a good time for me to share an emphatic statement: Of all the people we tried to get help from for our son, the sheriff's department officials offered us the most help, compassion, and support, not only during these difficult days, but in the days that were yet to come!

In the meantime our oldest son, Brad, whom Dave had called earlier, arrived and went to our neighbor's house and met up with Dave's older brother, Mike. Mike, along with Dave's dad and two other brothers, had all made the three-hour drive from southern Iowa. I can't imagine what thoughts were running through Brad's mind during that four-and-a-half-hour trip from South Dakota he had to make by himself that day.

What I remember most, though, is how our son, Scott, continued to lift everyone up in prayer. How is it that a seventeen-year-old had the presence of mind to help us all cope that day? My folks were desperate to be near us and were able to come in and give us a hug. My brother stayed with us. We were numb. It was surreal. This couldn't be happening.

When I hear about calamitous events such as what occurred in our community, I don't usually stop to think about the "other" side of the story. What I mean is that I often pray for the obvious people that are affected, but I don't go beyond that and consider the suffering that goes on with all the people affected by these tragedies. That is why some of my family have shared their thoughts about the impact that day had on them.

Here are some thoughts from Mark's Grandma Marlene:

My beloved grandson, Mark. Ray and I had just gotten home from daily mass at church when the phone rang and it was our son Michael. He called to tell us that Ed Thomas had been shot and that Mark did the shooting. Michael also said that he had called his aunt and uncle to come to our house so we wouldn't be alone. He made a second call to us to say that Ed had died.

My first feeling was total shock. I started screaming for Mark and tried not to believe it. Then the tears came and I couldn't stop. Ray had to hold on to me. I totally lost it. My legs wouldn't hold me.

My stomach hurt for days and weeks. After I settled down a little I just wanted to get to Joan and Dave and Scott, which we did. We met at the jail where they had taken Mark. Our son Michael was there too.

One thing I thank God for every day is that three days before this shooting Ray and I had seen Ed and Jan. We had a nice visit. I told them, "Thank you for supporting David and Joan as they are trying to get help for Mark." Ed just gave me a big hug and said, "Marlene, this is what Christian friends do for each other." He had tears in his eyes. Jan said, "Joan and David would be here in a second if it was one of our boys needing help."

Both my sister Sheryl and my twin sister, Jane, were traveling that day. Here are my sister Sheryl's thoughts from that day:

It had been a long time since I had taken a vacation. Several years in fact. I had just boarded my connecting flight in Chicago and was waiting for my friend to board. We were on our way to Sanibel, Florida, to spend five days with family and friends . . . hanging out on the beach, eating all the seafood I wanted, getting an unhealthy tan. I had waited a long time for this. I was settling into my seat when my phone rang. Rachel?? Why was my niece calling me on a Wednesday morning? I answered with a question in my voice, "Hey Rachel?" She responded, "Aunt Sheryl, Coach Thomas has been shot. They think it was Mark." My head started spinning. Was

Coach okay? Where were Dave and Joan and
Scott? Were they okay? Oh dear god, I had been
so afraid that something might happen to them.
I had been afraid Mark would hurt them . . . The
confusion was nauseating. My friend boarded the
plane. But he took one look at me and sat down
fast. I did not know what to do. Get off and fly
back? Go on to Florida and fly back? How was
my family? How was my sister? What happened
to Mark? What made him do this? My friend
convinced me to get to Tampa and take it from
there. I had to turn my phone off because the
plane was departing.

When we landed in Tampa I turned my
phone back on. And there was the message from
Rachel: "Coach Thomas is dead. Dave, Joan, and
Scott are in a safe place. Mark is in custody."

Here are some thoughts my twin sister Jane shared with me:

My cell phone was ringing. It was 5:30 a.m. I
was disoriented waking up in a strange hotel
room. We had been traveling for two, eleven-hour
days to get to Boise, Idaho, and we had almost
ten more hours to go to get to Eugene, Oregon,
today. Our daughter had qualified for the USA

Track & Field Championships again and we were so excited to go. I quickly got out of bed and went to an area where I could talk without waking up my husband and daughter. "Good morning, Jane!" came brightly over the line from my sister Joan. "Have you forgotten I am in Boise and we are an hour behind you?" I asked, chuckling. She quickly apologized but it didn't stop our conversation. As twin sisters we have started many of our mornings having a cup of coffee and conversation together over the years.

She was on her way to Ames to work for the day and during her drive time we were catching up. She explained to me that Mark had been released from the hospital the night before and was at home. I was confused. Shouldn't he be in jail? After the weekend before we were sure that the hospital would finally be keeping Mark long enough to diagnose what was going on with him. She said Mark told them no charges had been filed. Something was obviously wrong but they didn't have any answers yet. I asked her to call me and let me know what they found out and we ended our conversation.

I started getting ready and a short while later I received a call from my sister-in-law, Sherry. Now this was unusual. I answered the phone and immediately could tell from her voice that something was wrong. She asked me, "Have you talked to Joan this morning?" I replied that I had spoken to her earlier and said, "Why do you ask?" She replied, "Ed Thomas has been shot and they think Mark did it!"

Apparently at this point I screamed, "No!" and fell to the floor. My daughter, Rachel, tells me this but in my shock I do not have memory of it. I know Sherry said to me, "You have to come back, Joan will need you." I hung up the phone and found that my mind was reeling, trying to decide what to do. Should I fly back? Do we drive back? I need to talk to Joan . . . so much confusion. I tried to call Joan, but there was no answer. I called my brother, Mike, and explained where Joan's office was located so he could go to her. I have memories of my husband lying back on the bed. I know he was praying. I heard Rachel making phone calls, letting our other daughter and family members know.

We quickly packed up and hit the road. What a long twenty-two-hour drive that was. We alternately talked, prayed, and cried, but mostly were just quiet, each with our own thoughts. Why, why, why kept going through our minds. Sadly, there were no answers. As we were traveling during the night on I-80, I turned to my husband and said, "One thing is for sure, Satan has picked the wrong two families to attack this time. They will not turn away from their faith." Faith is the only thing that got us all through the days and nights that were yet to come.

It was late afternoon when we were finally driven to our home. I can shut my eyes and relive the drive in the DCI agent's vehicle from the county sheriff's department to our rural home, stopping just short of the blue Chevy Lumina blocking our path. The sheriff's deputy guarding the property stepped out of his car and spoke quietly with the agent before allowing us to proceed on foot. We trudged up the long winding driveway to our house, on legs that would barely carry us. The air was heavy with humidity, and the mosquitoes were buzzing in our ears.

The agent instructed us to gather a few belongings but not to touch anything in the house. Upon nervous entry to our home, I walked back to the bedroom to collect some clothes and toiletries. I honestly don't even know what I was throwing into the suitcase. My husband had stopped cold in the hallway just staring at the ceramic tile floor, looking at the mud that had been tracked in from our son's frantic pacing earlier that day, back and forth, back and forth. At the end of the hallway in our youngest son's bedroom hung a picture of our high school football coach with four of his former players that had made it to the NFL. My husband broke down and wept. We both broke down and wept.

We trekked back on foot to the agent's vehicle and he transported us to our neighbor's house, the safe house where our family had gathered to escape the media and curious onlookers. A caravan took us an hour away to our destination for the night. Meanwhile, back at home, law enforcement strangers spent most of the evening combing through our home for evidence.

Dave's brothers and dad, along with a host of my family, huddled together that night and we cried, prayed, and were in shock together. I was exhausted and couldn't really even think straight. Although my family was attempting to protect us from watching or hearing the news on TV, I couldn't help but hear the news coverage and see the pictures of our son plastered across the screen. This became a national news story overnight and I just wanted to call and scream to everyone that it wasn't Mark that committed this hideous act but a delusional insane mind!

I'll never forget the calm that came over me when I heard the news statement from Aaron Thomas about remembering to keep the Becker family in your prayers. The other peaceful memory of that night is the brief phone conversation Jan (Ed's wife) and I had that night. She wanted to assure me that she wasn't holding anything against our family and that she was separating what Mark did from us and that she just wanted me to know she was praying for us. I felt wholly inadequate as I, too, expressed my concern and sorrow for her and her family. I also told her I was praying for all of them.

When Dave and I finally got to bed that night we held each other tight. We were numb, exhausted, and heavyhearted. How could our son, who couldn't stand to even see an animal in pain, ever have taken the life of someone he respected so much? We knew it wasn't our son that performed that act, but a man who was in a delusional, psychotic, insane state. We knew this, but the world didn't know this. They hadn't lived the horror of the last ten to twelve months of psychotic episodes our family had endured. They didn't know the extent to which we had gone, trying to get help for our son. To have endured all of the prior months' pain, and then have it result in a tragedy such as this was inconceivable.

Sleep eventually did find me that night. I was having a nightmare about our son, Mark, doing something horrific and tragic. But when morning came, I woke up and realized it wasn't a nightmare—it was real, and my heart began to bleed.

9

AMAZING GRACE

What met us the next day when we returned home and over the weeks to come was God at work! Our families did not leave our side . . . and I still think back to their journeys from that horrific day. I believe my family must have set up a schedule of who would be staying with us because we were not left alone for a long time to come. Brad stepped right in and took over the job of protecting us from the media. He's a big guy, standing six feet three, and no one bothered us whatsoever. What they didn't know is that Brad is just a big teddy bear!

The day after we arrived home, my twin sister, Jane, and her family arrived. Jane and I are like one . . . and her presence made me break down completely but also gave me a strength that only a twin bond understands.

The days that followed became a whirlwind as hundreds of people came to our home to offer support and comfort to us. Everyone who came would hug me and say, "Jan says to tell you she is thinking of you." Cards

from all over the country started arriving in our mailbox.
Our mailman had to start bringing them up to our house
because the stack of cards was too big to fit in our mailbox.
Food and supplies were brought in by neighbors and
friends. Remember the community of Parkersburg I talked
about earlier? I think back to the devastating tornado that
rocked our small town and remember how God worked in
everyone's lives during that time. Both the Parkersburg and
Aplington—the small town four miles west of Parkersburg—
communities banded together during that time. In a way, I
believe God was preparing all of us for yet another tragedy to
befall us. Recalling how everyone rallied around the Thomas
family, as well as our family, speaks volumes to me of how
great the people we live amongst are.

A few days after the tragedy I woke up really early, or
perhaps I had not slept. I was hurting so badly. I had been
praying for Jan . . . over and over again. My head throbbed
with the pain I felt for Ed's family. I couldn't escape it.
Around 5:00 a.m. I showered and called my twin sister who
was staying at her mother-in-law's house in Parkersburg. I
told her I needed her help to do something. I had her drive
me to Cedar Falls where I picked up a beautiful flowering
plant for Jan. There was something else I needed to find. I
had to go a couple places searching for it, but I finally found
it—a bleeding heart plant. That plant explained how I was
feeling . . . my heart was bleeding for Ed, for Jan, for their
sons, for their grandchildren, and for their families. It was

also bleeding for Mark, our family, our extended families, our church members, the school where Ed taught, our communities of Parkersburg and Aplington and everyone else affected by the loss of Ed.

It was hard listening to a conversation at the greenhouse checkout between two men talking about my son Mark. One of them stated, "That guy must be crazy!" I think my sister Jane wanted to interrupt them and say something but I nudged her and shook my head. I just wanted to get the plant and get out of there.

As we drove back to Parkersburg and Jane drove me to Jan's house, I prayed that Jan would see me. I didn't want to cause her any more pain. As I started walking to the house, I stumbled. It was like my legs would not carry me. One of Jan's sons was outside, and he and my sister helped me into the house. I told Jan I couldn't go another day without seeing her and talking to her. God gave me such a peace when I was able to cry with Jan as I tried to use words to say how sorry I was. How do you explain the ache a heart bears for another in such a situation? We just hugged each other, both of us hurting so deeply. No words can express the thoughts and emotions during a time such as this.

I'll never forget the grace we received from Jan Thomas and her family. Pastor Brad was visiting Dave and me at our home. I asked him if we could attend the visitation and funeral for Ed. He then talked to Jan about it and she not only said yes, but she made special arrangements for our family to attend the visitation privately before anyone else. I'll never forget the comfort it gave to our family when Dave, Brad, Scott, and I could say good-bye to Ed in private. We were able to talk to Jan, Aaron, and Todd personally with no one else around. One of the funeral home attendants came up and quietly said, "Jan, we need to start letting people in." Jan calmly replied, "You give the Beckers as much time as they need." Thank you, Jan, . . . thank you.

I think of how this tragedy affected my husband, a lot. That day he lost his former football coach, he lost a mentor, he lost a fellow deacon, he lost a Sunday school teacher, and he lost a friend. But Dave, in a sense, lost a son that day too. Even though Mark had an illness, we never gave up hope believing he would get a diagnosis and medication so he could live a normal life. How is it possible, after years of trying to get our son help, that it would result in the loss of life like this?

The result of a tragedy is felt by many. Not only does it affect the victim's immediate family, but their extended family, friends, community, church members, and business colleagues. What is often forgotten is the family of the one who did the act itself. Our families have suffered deeply and in silence.

Here are some thoughts shared by Mark's first cousin, Mandy:

Amazing Grace

"Things like this don't happen to families like ours."

Call it arrogance or ignorance, I don't know, but that is all I could think as I sat frozen at my desk, staring unseeing at my computer. My mom had just called me at work in a panic. I couldn't take it in. It was too unbelievable. Seriously! Things like this didn't happen to families like ours.

In the days and weeks that followed the world seemed different. Scarier. Colder. Unsure. It hadn't changed, I had. The cute conversations my two-year-old would have with herself now became panic inducing. Was it normal or some early sign of schizophrenia?

In many ways my life has two parts. Before the shooting and after. No matter the changes we have endured, God has proven his steadfastness. He is still sovereign. He is still loving. He still offers hope through his son. At this point some people might say something like, "I wouldn't change a thing." I'm not going to say that. If given the choice I'd change everything. I'd change Mark's mental illness. I'd change the pain my aunt, uncle, cousins, and extended family bear. I'd give back the husband, father, and grandfather to the Thomases. But I can't.

God's will is not my own. Our family has suffered
and there are wounds that will not be healed
this side of heaven, but that does not change
the fact that God's will is perfect. We might not
understand it but there is always hope through
Jesus Christ and for that I am thankful—thankful
that through God's grace this tragedy is not
for nothing. Mark's suffering, our suffering, the
Thomases' suffering . . . it is not in vain.

That following year, one of the best healing forces was
that our son Scott was a senior in high school. I honestly
wonder if Dave and I hadn't had all of Scott's activities to
attend that year if we would have ever been brave enough to
venture into town. It was like God knew we would need that
busy year with Scott to begin the healing process.

We have been overwhelmed by the support from our
family, the church, the school, the community, and people
all over the country, as they have reached out to comfort us
in the aftermath of that horrific "storm" of June 24, 2009.
Everywhere I go people ask me if the local community has
really been as good to us as the media makes them out to
be. Yes, I respond, yes they have. We will never forget the
outpouring of love and support they provided at that time
and even today. They have *all* helped our family begin to see
a glimmer of light beyond the storm.

10

THE VICTIM OF A VICTIM

I t was several long weeks before we were able to go and see Mark. He had been transferred to the Cerro Gordo County Jail at Mason City. We didn't know what to expect that first visit. We were apprehensive about seeing Mark. Would he be in an episode, would he be angry, would he be delusional? Dave and I had been praying constantly for our son and we had an hour on the trip north that night to summon help from God to give us strength.

When we arrived at the jail we learned the drill of visitor rules: show your ID, sign in, take a seat, and wait to see Mark until there was a visitor's booth open.

Tears sprung to our eyes as we watched Mark, who was in a straitjacket because of suicide watch, come and take a seat on the other side of the glass. He looked incredibly tired with dark circles under his eyes. As we picked up the phone to communicate through the glass to Mark on the other side, he seemed determined to get his first words out of his mouth:

"Mom and Dad, I'm so thankful you are alive. I believed God told me to kill Ed and you two that day so you would quit poisoning the minds of the children in our community." The chills that went down my spine when I heard those words spoken by my son are inexplicable. Mark went on to say that the psychologist had encouraged him to talk to us and to communicate as best he could. It did not go unnoticed by Dave and me the way Mark was furtively looking around— behind him, to his left, to his right. I came right out and asked him if he was hearing voices and having delusions.

"Yes, but they are giving me medicine that they say will help." He told us that a minister had visited him and prayed with him the first night he was taken to jail. Knowing that brought me so much relief. Just knowing my son wasn't completely alone with the horrifying aftermath of what he had been involved with helped me tremendously.

Our fifteen-minute time limit ended much too quickly, but we could see that the visit had exhausted Mark. We prayed with him before I blew him a kiss, told him I loved him, and said a tearful good-bye. This began the pattern of our visits over the next eight months as we awaited the upcoming trial.

The sheriff's department contracted with a facility to provide psychiatric services for inmates. They kept working with Mark until they could find the right combination of medications to reduce the effects of paranoid schizophrenia. It took about six months before we could tell that Mark was not struggling as much with the voices and delusions. We visited Mark every week and prayed with him and told him we loved him.

In preparation for the upcoming trial, Dave and I were interviewed by psychologists and psychiatrists. One particular question Dave and I had for these professionals was about Mark's prior drug use. The answer was always the same. No, drug use did not *cause* Mark's paranoid schizophrenia. No, drug use certainly did not *help* Mark's illness. However, Mark states to us today, "I hope people that read your book realize they shouldn't use drugs, but that they *do* need to take the medications doctors prescribe to them for their illness."

Dave and I have since talked around and around about Mark's childhood and constantly tried to figure out why Mark suffers from this mental illness. Yes, we do have other family members that cope with depression, bipolar, and paranoid schizophrenia. But anyone who has a loved one with a mental illness puts themselves through a period of second-guessing their parenting skills, the childhood illnesses, and accidents along the way.

Dave and I remembered a particular time when Mark was just an infant. It was September 1985 and I decided we needed a weekend adventure visiting my brother's family in Wisconsin. When I say *we*, I really mean *me*, as in I needed to get out of the house and get away! My husband didn't quite buy into the work it took to pack up two babies and all of the absolute necessities of life and drive six hours in a 1981 two-door Chevy Citation. But, as is quite often the case, Dave humored me and off we went.

I felt alive as I helped chop veggies in my sister-in-law's kitchen while she cooked up the meal. Adult conversation was awesome and just what I needed. Mark was strapped into his infant seat and had an eye-level view of me as I worked. As he bounced and entertained himself, he suddenly propelled himself forward, his weight jerking the infant seat to the ceramic tile floor. My heart sunk to my stomach and I felt like my body was in slow motion as I tried to stop the fall. I instantly unstrapped Mark and held him close and searched for injuries. Off to the hospital we went.

I was sweaty after hours of holding Mark in the hot, stuffy waiting room. The doctor finally examined him and explained that although right now he didn't see any concerns there could be brain injuries due to the fall and it could be adulthood before anything would come to light. This was little consolation to a mother who already felt guilt pressing down on her shoulders. How could I have let this happen to my baby? Only time would tell.

The professionals kept telling Dave and me not to blame ourselves for what Mark did or for Mark's illness, but it has taken a very long time to convince ourselves of that.

Although we, his parents, knew Mark was not sane when he shot Ed Thomas, I don't believe in my heart I ever expected a jury to understand that. They didn't know the struggles we had gone through trying to get Mark help. They didn't know the psychotic episodes our family had been experiencing for a year. They didn't know Mark is one of the gentlest people you would ever know. How could they? All the jury was exposed to was the monster that emerged that fateful day in June. But here is the bottom line: God knows and we, Mark's parents, know quite simply that Mark would never kill anyone in his sane mind.

The trial was agonizing for everyone: the Thomas family, for our family, and for those poor students who had to relive their nightmare of being in the weight room that fateful day. When the jury was wrestling with determining the verdict, I wrote the following statement because this was what I was going to say no matter what the verdict turned out to be. I wanted people to understand that Mark was a victim of a failed mental health system and, as a result, the entire Thomas family became victims as well. In fact, our family became victims of that failed system too. It didn't have to be that way!

Press Release from Joan and David Becker
2/24/2010

The last weeks, months, and years have been extremely difficult for our family to bear. We have watched our son Mark go from being a handsome, fun-loving young man who even brought his brother Scott to Christ many years ago . . . to a frightened lonely person trying to fight off demons too numerous for any of us to ever understand.

Our son Mark Becker would never take the life of another person if he was of sane mind!

Ed Thomas was a victim of a victim. Although Mark and we, as his parents, attempted to go through all the right channels to get Mark the mental health treatment he so desperately needed, the system failed miserably!

Our sorrow runs so deep . . . for the family of Ed Thomas, for our church family, for our community, for our own families but most of all for our son Mark whom we love so much.

We appreciate the respect the media has given our family during this most difficult of times. We appreciate the job everyone has done during this trial process . . . especially the jury. I cannot imagine being able to separate emotion from the law in making the decision they had to make today.

God is with us; God will give us strength to move forward and heal; and we will continue to give God the glory.

Mark was sentenced to life in prison. Dave and I consistently prayed for God's will throughout the trial. We knew Mark would never live with us at home again. We knew Mark would never realize the dream of being a husband or a father. All of our hopes and aspirations for our middle son seem to have vanished. So what do we do with this?

Everyone who faces a storm such as this has a choice: you can hide out where it is safe or you can speak out in an effort to help others. Dave and I prayed about how God could use our family's journey to help others. This is why I publicly share our story to help advocate for those who are walking down the dark alley of mental illness.

Many of you are reading this book for different reasons. If you are an individual who suffers from an illness of the brain, I want you to know I earnestly pray for you. I want the stigma of this illness to be erased from our society so that you can be open about your illness if you choose to be.

If you are a family member or caregiver of someone with an illness of the brain, my heart and prayers go out to you as well. It is a never-ending battle you must wage each and every day to fight for those you love.

If you are someone who works in the mental health field, a counselor, caseworker, psychologist, psychiatrist, staff person, nurse, and the list goes on and on, do not just go through the motions of your job. *Listen* to the patient and the patient's caregivers. If you choose to work in this field, give it everything you've got. When these individuals and families finally make the step to seek help, remember that they have already been through so much grief and anguish. You affect people's lives with every decision you make. Every one of us has to be willing to use the gifts God has given us to our fullest potential. When we get to the point that we are emotionally and physically exhausted from giving our job the best we possibly can, then maybe we need to have the grace and wisdom to pursue another gift in life.

If you are someone in law enforcement, the court system, or the judicial system, remember that just because someone made mistakes or poor choices in the past, it does not mean they should be written off for the rest of their life. There just might be some serious health condition which caused these poor decisions in the first place.

If you have been elected to serve as a representative or senator, state or federal, and have taken on the responsibility to serve your citizens, you have the power to fund programs to help make our mental health system viable, strong, and accountable. I'm not necessarily saying you have to throw tons more money toward it; I'm just saying there needs to be oversight to make sure the money is being spent wisely and that it is providing services to the individuals who so desperately need them.

The above list of people covers hundreds of thousands of people, if not millions. So you see, each and every one of us bear a responsibility to make a better system and world for those who have an illness of the brain. So, what are *you* going to do about it?

11

FINDING THE LIGHT
BEYOND THE STORM

When each of my boys was born, I had a conversation with God about what an awesome responsibility he had given to Dave and me with the gift of a child. I knew that God had placed us in our role as parents to simply do the best we could each and every day. That is, by faith, what we have attempted to do.

As I said early on in this book, my husband and I felt strongly about attending church together as a family. During the trial we saw firsthand what the support of a church body can do. They provided meals to both the Thomas and Becker families throughout the trial. They also had a prayer schedule set up so our families would be lifted up in prayer throughout the entire trial. We received an outpouring of support from our family, friends, and community. I'll always remember the shawl a women's group from a neighboring church prayed over as they knitted it for me. My sister gave it to me when we got home after the trial one day. As I wrapped it around my shoulders such peace came over me. To this day I use that prayer shawl and it continues to give me a peace, comfort, and warmth. And then there was a basket my fellow workers prepared for our family. It was not only full of snacks and goodies, but each person had handwritten a note of support and encouragement for our family. This meant so much to Dave and me, and to our entire family.

Our family attended the same church as the Thomas family. We continued to attend this church for quite some time after this tragedy. However, there came a day when my husband came to the car and found me, yet again, sobbing. I explained to him that in order for me to heal I needed to move forward and begin attending a different church. I love the church family at the church where Dave and I grew in our faith both individually and as a couple. But to continue to see that empty seat by Jan, Ed's wife, was too much for me. There was a church in a neighboring town that had actually called us after the tragedy. They said they had prayed about what they could do to help the individuals involved. God prompted that church to reach out to our family and offer counseling, which they did. This is the church my husband and I attend today. I have been able to forgive, heal, and start to get involved again with God's purpose for me. I miss the people from our former church, and they are forever in my heart and prayers.

What I found to be so profound, throughout the interviews that took place with ESPN, ESPY, CBN 700 Club, local news stations, and newspapers, were the caring hearts of everyone involved. When you see many of these crew members moved to tears during the interviews that took place, you know their hearts have been touched.

Forgiveness is essential for and by each one of us. It has taken me some time, but there are many people I have had to forgive: Mark, the doctors who I *thought* failed Mark, those who criticized my son after this tragedy, and everyone else involved in the mental health system including attorneys, judges, law enforcement, and agencies. Speaking publicly and sharing our family's personal story has not only helped bring awareness of the gaps that exist in our mental health system, but it has also taught me a lot about the roadblocks our mental health system faces trying to do their jobs.

It is interesting how many people, including attorneys, have listened to our family's story and asked, "Why haven't you filed any lawsuits?" Here is the very simple answer to that question: Dave and I prayed about this and God's answer has been clear. We believe that the public sharing of our family's story will make a far bigger impact in people's lives and our mental health system than any lawsuit would do. Another very important aspect to our decision is this: Ed Thomas was emphatic that he did not approve of lawsuits and mentioned many times over the years in our Sunday school classes that he felt there was always a better way to resolve issues than by the use of lawsuits.

Mark is serving a life sentence. At the time of writing this book, Mark is housed at the Iowa Medical and Classification Center. He does receive treatment and medication (currently Seroquel) for paranoid schizophrenia. It is not an easy road, as those of you who live with a brain illness know, but we take it one day at a time. There are some periods where Mark just seems like the Mark of younger years. There are periods where he still struggles from the demons within. And there are periods where he doesn't want us to visit. That is the most heartbreaking time for me. I want to be able to hug him and remind him of our love for him, but sometimes it's just too painful for him to see us.

Mark fills his days with work, reading, drawing, playing guitar, and would also like to begin woodworking. I never realized that Mark's gifts would be so critical in his life ahead. Mark has shared many personal statements with us, but most of those I will leave for him to tell in his own time. But if I could pass one thing on from Mark, just know this: Mark is deeply sorry for what he did.

God never told us it was going to be an easy journey, but he does assure us the journey will be well worth it in the end.

Mark and I communicate through handwritten letters and also through email. He has shared many thoughts, some very deep, over the past few years. Here is one where he is trying to explain what goes through his mind during the delusional episodes. Mark has given permission to me to share the following with you, the reader:

Finding the Light Beyond the Storm

From: Mark Becker

Date: 7/24/2013 3:03:44 PM

Subject: I've been wrong

Message: I have had quite the day so far. Now I believe I was paranoid about everything lately. What should I say? I apologize.

Let me clear my head for a while, then I'll write again. It's kind of foggy right now. I'm not sure what's what or who's right. Sometimes I do hear things, but I'm so used to it it's boring. Sometimes I do imagine things. Sometimes I do see things that I don't understand but want to understand. I'm used to seeing things. I also realized that ever since I could remember, way back a long time ago, I would hear things and see things. But it was never as intense as when I moved back from South Dakota. It just got superamplified when we were driving in the car that day back to Iowa, remember that? I got scared when I didn't understand the sounds and images coming into my perception. Really scared!

When I kept hearing the same blaring shrill voice of Ed, it got under my skin and I kept acting like it wasn't there. Then when I realized it had been going on for nine months, I got sick of it, so I made my mind up to react. I didn't know what to do. I didn't know why everyone thought

I was sick. This has been in me since I was born. It just surfaces later in a higher intensity. I also hear Dad's voice and see Dad a lot. He is always taking a new form and angle in my perceptions of him. Why does he say what he says? Why does he show himself the way I see him? When will he be satisfied with what he's working on? Will what these people I see and hear ever be accomplished? Is there even a reason for it?

When I hear Dad and Ed's and Brad's and other's voices and see them showing themselves, what am I to do? If I react, I will be sick in the head. If I have mood swings, I will be heavily medicated. If I talk about it the wrong way, I will be punished. I don't want things to change, right now I am happy with where I'm at and my dose of medication is the best I can get it at.

I don't believe anyone can help me by talking to me, I don't believe any medications will improve my condition. No person knows what they are talking about, and that's what I believe firmly. I have to realize and know there is so much I will not understand, and there will always be a chaos element in life. Blessed and cursed are we all.

I hope this will help heal any wounds I have opened and have been denying since whenever.

Finding the Light Beyond the Storm

We all go around this carousel and I believe no one is left out. So I keep traveling the path. I do get scared, feel brave again, then exist. I don't expect anyone to open up to me, I don't even care. But this email is my way of confessing.

So download this letter and enjoy what it offers. You will notice after you read it you knew this all along. Thanks for being in my life, Mom. When can we see each other and hug and talk and catch up face-to-face? After that, I would like to see how I feel and how the sounds and sights are. So let's try it again, just me and you. What do ya say?

Mark

EPILOGUE

Everyone faces storms in life. Perhaps you have encountered a severe atmospheric or environmental storm like a hurricane, tornado, flood, or earthquake. The aftermath of such storms are traumatic and can cause lifelong effects in your life. Or what about the personal storms that come, uninvited, into your life? Is it the loss of a child, mother, or father? Or the insidious cancer that invades you or your loved one? Or a child gone astray? How do we survive the storm? How do we ever find the light in our lives again?

I still experience days when the devastating storm of June 24, 2009 assaults every one of my senses. But I am not alone. Every one of us will face storms in life. It is how we respond to them and claw our way out of them that is important. You *can* and *will* find the light again. Never give up hope, never give up trying, and never give up working to make a difference in someone else's life.

Mark still struggles with paranoid schizophrenia today, and always will. In this letter he wrote in October 2013 you can see how he continues to seek the answers within:

Dave & Joan,

Hello Mom & Dad! I'm writing now to clear up a few things. Here are the points of interest of concern . . .

Regarding my beliefs and religious views; please know I in no way whatsoever intended to push them on you. My last correspondences were wrong & unnecessary in every way! Who am I to do that to any person who is not interested to begin with? Sorry about it, let's move past the push and controlling past that I was very sickened with for an eternity it seems now. Now that I look in the mirror I ask myself who I am now? I try and peel back the mystery, the veil, to see the real person in there. I know the thing I see: a changed man.

Now my life is positive, free to be me and let go of the grudges against so many that I've held forever. My problems are laid out for me to resolve once and for all. And no person could ever get through to me all this time. I had too much baggage and no focus to mindfully deal with my inner reckonings and emotions. Much

Epilogue

comparable to an open face fishing reel that became all tangled & balled up in knots. Or something like the times one loses an object that was merely misplaced during the humdrum typical everyday living . . . it took a while!

So where do I find the solution when it hurts so bad I forgot I was made, forgot I was sad, and forgot who I am? I am now beginning to rediscover the root of my very being. I do have a family and extended family too. I discovered more than I knew, because I gave myself a chance, instead of giving up, to find the missing essence, what's inside. It's not in a song or a book. And we can all relate about money's grip and fast-paced ways. Before it's earned, it's spent on something isn't it? And our world . . .

What about living in America can we really strive for?

What are we working for, what are we collectively investing in?

How does our investment look in long-term value?

Are we making a place for our families to flourish in, or just destroying a place to live?

My questions are important to me, and I want you to tell me what you have thought about after you read this letter . . . and also as

my family it means something of value to me.
What you value.

I want to express something to you, the
Folks who raised me: I believe in the family
and the values our forefathers had long ago
before everything got fancy. When men and
government were all in harmony with the entire
world. Nature has become something put in
the backseat of priority, with our countrymen
treated more as contemptuous BUGS! I just have
to express that we are not BUGS! We are all
honorable in this web of existence, and we do
have a chance to become godly. Enough—

Please come to visit when you can. I am no
longer afraid of you. And I think we should catch
up, it's been too long!

Destiny becomes an absolute for every living
kinsman . . . for every leaf falls at winter's time,
not a one be spared. And tears fall as rain, for
me & you. Winter's sure as I and you. And so is
spring's flower.

Mark Daryl Becker

Here is a letter I wrote to Mark after a particularly heart-
wrenching letter (too deep for this book) came from him:

Epilogue

Dear Mark,

It's Saturday and I am alone in the house. I read your letter of October 22, 2013, for the fourth time . . . I read it out loud and sobbed through most of it.

The outpouring you write in words breaks my heart all over again. It brings back memories through my brain of every cry for help you waged to us. I can shut my eyes and it's like video clips of every single psychotic episode fly through my conscience . . . in the house, the car, the gazebo, on the farm. The nights we were up all night just to listen to you . . . not understanding what you were living and experiencing but trying so desperately to understand.

Yes, we did recognize your cry for help, but did not know how to answer that plea from you. Do you know that no one knows how to answer that cry? No one knows the "why" of paranoid schizophrenia, Mark. The doctors and medicines are really just feeble attempts to try and help.

I ask you this . . . how do you think it feels to a Mom and Dad to see and experience our son's absolute terror and suffering and for us to have no clue as to how to help you? To this day I still struggle with that very question . . . and

SENTENCED TO **LIFE**

I will continue to struggle with the guilt and "what ifs" my entire life. The public speaking and the writing of my book is therapy for me. I keep desperately trying to help others, all the while knowing I couldn't even help my own son.

This failure as a mother kills me, Mark . . . but I will never give up hoping and praying for a miracle. A miracle for you and a miracle for others who suffer this tormented life.

Please, my son, know this . . . I love you and everything I do today, and I did in the past, was based on that love. I am not perfect, I do not have all the answers, I do not know how to help you . . . but I will never give up trying!

Mark, thank you for sharing and exposing your innermost thoughts. The world needs to know the torment you continue to live with each and every day.

My love to my son forever and always,

Mom

RESOURCES

If you or someone you know is struggling with signs of a brain illness, seek help immediately! Do *not* let the stigma of our society get in the way of recognizing the importance of early diagnosis. Ask for a release of information form to be signed so you can be an active part of your loved one's treatment.

If you are experiencing anything close to what I've described in our family's story, *get help now!* Call your local governmental authority who helps connect those with mental illness to the service providers, call your local law enforcement, contact someone at your church, call your local medical doctor . . . just keep calling and asking for help until *someone* can point you in the right direction. Don't assume things will get better, because they will not.

Support Organizations

- NAMI – National Alliance on Mental Illness: www.nami.org
- MHA – Mental Health America: www.mentalhealthamerica.net
- Bring Change 2 Mind – www.bringchange2mind.org
- American Psychiatric Association – www.psychiatry.org/home

Recognizing Early Warning Signs of Mental Illnesses

The American Psychiatric Association (APA) provides an excellent online article explaining the warning signs of mental illness. This link will take you to the APA website: http://www.psych.org/mental-health/more-topics/warning-signs-of-mental-illness.